Janet Lynn Roseman

The V
of th
Woman Writer

Pre-publication
REVIEW

"**I** was moved, inspired, and heartened to read Janet Roseman's passionate guide for women. To reclaim a life, to mine its depths and discover its truths, read this book. It is a treasure."

Sherry Ruth Anderson, PhD
Psychologist; Co-author,
The Feminine Face of God

The Way of the Woman Writer

HAWORTH Innovations in Feminist Studies
Esther Rothblum, PhD and Ellen Cole, PhD
Senior Co-Editors

New, Recent, and Forthcoming Titles:

The Way of the Woman Writer

Janet Lynn Roseman, MS

Harrington Park Press
An Imprint of The Haworth Press, Inc.
New York • London • Norwood (Australia)

Published by

Harrington Park Press, an imprint of The Haworth Press, Inc., 10 Alice Street, Binghamton, NY 13904-1580

Library of Congress Cataloging-in-Publication Data

Roseman, Janet Lynn.
  The way of the woman writer / Janet Lynn Roseman.
    p. cm.
  Includes bibliographical references and index.
  ISBN 1-56023-860-7 (pbk. : alk paper).
  1. Authorship–Sex differences. 2. Women and literature. 3. Women authors. I. Title.
PN171.S45R67 1994
808'.02'082–dc20   94-22764
                                                                                          CIP

About six months before I began to write this book, I had a dream. The dream was filled with images which are difficult to explain in words. What I do remember, however, is that I was told in the dream to write down the following phrase: "Janet, you are part of the women who have lived and loved before you." This book is dedicated to those women.

To Minnie Roseman, my grandmother, who never had the opportunity to tell her story.

ABOUT THE AUTHOR

Janet Lynn Roseman, MS, teaches journalism and English classes at several San Francisco Bay Area universities. She is a dance critic and specializes in writing interviews and entertainment articles for national and international publications. She is the author of *Gumps Since 1861: A San Francisco Legend.* Currently, she is writing books on the craft of women writers, theVirgin Mary, and women artists from the 1920s.

CONTENTS

Foreword

When I was first attempting to write a text to accompany the unpublished Motherpeace Tarot cards (co-created in the late 1970s with Karen Vogel), I was writing in the common jargon of Tarot at the time, which was old fashioned and totally unsuited to contemporary feminist's lives. A publisher in New York, seriously considering the cards and the accompanying book, said to me: "Your writing is so strong, but what are you talking about???" It was only after our failure to attain a publisher (they decided the cards were not "cost effective") that we decided to publish them ourselves.

Fatefully, several months after self-publishing the cards, an editor at Harper San Francisco wrote me and offered to publish my book! Since the cards were now printed in full color, to write the book I simply placed each card in front of me as I sat at my typewriter, and with my resource books all around me, I would begin to write. It was brilliant. The information I had researched organized itself into coherent expressions of what I wanted to say, but in a language that was conversational and intelligible, because I was "channeling" it from what the cards were communicating to me. The awkward and lofty language of the Tarot genre could be left behind naturally, replaced by my authentic voice and genuine authority. I can still use the book today as an oracle for myself!

So I was quite struck by the fact that one of Janet Roseman's main teaching techniques is this "trick" of first drawing a picture of what you have in mind to write, and then writing from the picture. Somehow the mind and all its deadly sabotage can be circumvented through this and other childlike and marvelous processes. Roseman uses visualization and meditation techniques throughout this simple and direct handbook for (potential) women writers. Affirming and utilizing women's natural abilities as strengths–intuition, instinct, feelings, senses, and life experience–rather than weaknesses, she encourages women to be who they are and not disguise or hide their true selves in their writing.

The book recreates what it must be like to take Janet Roseman's writing classes, where she focuses on the particular problems and skills of women attempting to learn the art of putting thought to paper. Her loving approach to women is demonstrated in a sustained effort to draw out of them their own sense of self, and to instill in them an authentic female authority that their culture has denied. I almost felt as if I were getting to know the various characters in a novel, as she uses samples of the writing from her students to illustrate each exercise she offers the reader. The women's voices are at times shy and innocent, at other times surprisingly direct and the written pieces quite moving.

Throughout the book, Roseman suggests ways and means of reaching deep levels where the Muse can speak, and evoking the courage needed to speak from the inner self to the world. Women's special difficulties–the hideous "voluntary restraint" of our voices, our fears, self-doubt, busyness, and tendency to put others always first–are intelligently addressed by a woman who has clearly found her way through these obstacles. In a time when women's voices are desperately needed if our world is to survive, Janet Roseman's book is a helping hand in the direction of female authority and leadership.

Vicki Noble

There is an internal landscape, a geography of the soul; we search for its outlines all our lives. Those who are lucky enough to find it ease like water over a stone, onto its fluid contours, and are home.

–Josephine Hart, *Damage,*
(New York, Alfred Knopf, 1991, pg. 1).

Preface

ON WRITING WOMEN'S AUTOBIOGRAPHY

Countless diaries, journals, and letters that women have written for themselves, to friends, family, and lovers have been hidden and discarded in trunks and wastepaper baskets. Important fragments, pieces of women's lives lie silently screaming for our attention. Many of these pages secretly rest inside women's dresser drawers. Excavating the contents of these documents could be quite astonishing. Jean Cocteau believed that, "Every time we write, every blot on paper composes our self-portrait to denounce us." I disagree. I believe that every line a woman writes announces her. Perhaps it is that very fear of announcing herself that summons her to begin writing and causes her to halt in her tracks before nary a word is penned.

Writing offers us a powerful form to recount our personal mythology. By engaging in the process of writing about our lives, we can examine, invent, and re-invent ourselves anew with greater understanding. Resurrecting our internal landscape onto paper is both compelling and addictive to those who accept the challenge inherent in the process of writing a woman's life.

However, to view, to experience, and to understand what we have written on paper is not a static process. The reality that presents itself on paper is only a reflection of our lives *at that moment*. We are in charge of the content, and we can change it by the stroke of our pens.

Our lives are mutable and fluid, always shifting, becoming clearer, then murky, then clear again. This dance between murkiness and clarity continues throughout our lives and holds great beauty and power for each woman. Our histories, our experiences call to us, always speaking our truths in a deep and resonant voice; it only asks us to listen. Only when women have the courage to write their stories, to write their truths, to address their silences, only then can their authentic journeys begin.

Many of the grand traditions of autobiography have been lost and forgotten primarily because of its form; the oral autobiography. Native American women, African-American women, women emigres from all nations have always shared their truth stories and the stories of the women who came before them through the oral tradition. When women came together to weave baskets, to quilt, to cook a meal, to share a cup of coffee, or to work on an assembly line, their stories emerged.

This legacy from grandmother to granddaughter, from sister to sister, from mother to daughter, from woman friend to woman friend, from co-worker to co-worker, from lover to lover, has always been a natural channel for telling a woman's life. Because women's stories have been lost, the art of women's autobiography, oral or written, is elevated every time a woman declares her story, speaks her truth, and addresses her silence.

Women's narrative carries with it a rich history. African-American women slaves, women pioneers, and gypsy women wrote, spoke, and published their stories. Storytellers from all cultures passed on their mother's teachings and the teachings of their culture through narrative. Unfortunately, the rich vibrancy of oral autobiography lives only for the moment inside of the woman who tells of her grandmother's and her great-grandmother's experiences. We easily share our own experiences when we gather to honor a woman's rites of passage: the move to a new home, a new marriage, the birth of a child, or a new career. Women have always told their truths, sometimes with joy, sometimes in shame, sometimes with love.

Oral history has been denigrated, devalued, and discounted in the same ways women's writing has been. Countless academic treatises dismiss women's autobiography as insignificant compared to "real writing." (What is not said but implied is "real men's writing.") This devaluing of women's words is integrated into our culture. It's no wonder women are hesitant to speak or write about their lives.

Women's writing in general, including women's autobiographical writing, is frequently ignored. It makes perfect sense to me that many women writers in the nineteenth and twentieth centuries chose to publish by using male pseudonyms; they had little opportunity to publish their works under their own names without being criticized and ostracized.

Women's autobiography is still considered "confessional," a term that not only belittles women, but instantly dismisses their lives as not valid. The word, "confessional," is a derogatory term when used in conjunction with women's writing because it implies that the writing is something "less than." When women write their experiences on paper, when they resist the urge to make their writing pretty, when they remove the veils and respect their work, they take the first steps in honoring their life experiences.

It is curious to me that the criticism that accompanies this "confessional writing" theory also includes statements that women's writing is "too real" and "too authentic." Male autobiography may be criticized on other points; however, it is never considered "confessional writing." Malcolm X's autobiography had its critics, but I do not recall "confessional writing" being cited as a problem.

Many women writers and would-be writers are stymied before they even pick up their pens. When any culture refuses to acknowledge the power of women's voices and words, or any voice for that matter, everyone suffers. There is so much to be gained by the sharing of stories, knowledge, education, and ultimately, a mutual recognition of our humanness. When those stories are lost or thwarted, those opportunities are stolen. If women continue to hide their writing because they believe that it is only "confessional," then they lose contact with not only the words, but themselves.

I began offering women's autobiography workshops because I was more and more distressed by the comments that I would hear from the women students in my writing classes. Their chants of, "It's just about me; it is boring." "This is stupid; it's about my recent divorce." "I don't think this is any good; it's about my mother and me," troubled me. They devalued not only their own writing, but they also devalued their own lives, as if what they had experienced did not count.

The women students' apologized repeatedly about their work, and it was most disturbing to me. It also touched a raw nerve inside of me. I couldn't believe it. They were the architects of their own lives; and yet they didn't trust their own voices, their own words.

I was sad. I was angry. I knew I would try to do something. My doubting voice lived inside me, too. In the workshops, I encouraged my students to write about what they saw, experienced, or felt, for I believe that is the only way to become a true writer. When you write about what is true in your life, what is authentic, and what you have survived, then you are the expert, and the writing can be trusted. Judging by the wide spectrum of words that I have read over the years, it is only when the writer finds her truth that she is in touch with her own writing voice.

I thought that if I offered classes in women's autobiography that were safe and supportive, something magical could happen. It did. The women discovered themselves, healed themselves, and learned to trust their writing as guides back to themselves.

Monday evenings held a special place in my week. A small group of women, twenty to sixty-five years of age, used to gather in my Russian Hill apartment for a few hours to share their writing, their visions and their stories.

The group met faithfully for over three years and was one of the most exciting and revealing experiences that I have ever had the privilege of participating in. I decided to call the class, "Telling Tales: Women Write Autobiography." I wanted to work with women who felt as if their voice didn't count, who felt silenced. I wanted my students to develop a greater sense of themselves and a greater love of themselves, and to realize that they were, indeed, writers.

I was very fortunate, for over the years, I have had the pleasure of working with a number of extremely talented women. They have taught me as much as I have taught them, and I am most grateful. When they would seize the power existing in their words, I would listen and witness their transformation. I have had the chance to learn about women much different from myself . . . nuns, retired women, women with children, gay women, women from all stations in life. It was a very meaningful and profound opportunity.

I know now, listening to other women writers, that the documentation of their lives and the process of writing was not only crucial, but it gave me strength and encouragement in my work and my life. We all have the choice to honor our writing and use it as a powerful vehicle if we are willing to write the truth, not pen "pretty autobiography" as many of the how-to-write-your-life-story books espouse.

These books are not only insipid, they are dangerous for they lead us away from ourselves.

Writing one's life takes courage, but it is rich in its rewards. Women's autobiography is accessible and available to all who are willing to take the plunge to listen to themselves and to believe in what they write. You can trust your own words. Don't let anyone tell you differently.

Writing women's autobiography is a journey, an adventure, and an evolving practice. Anais Nin believed that women writers needed to find their own way, to find what she called, "the women's way," and I agree. Have faith, trust yourself and your words. Seek to find your own way.

Acknowledgements

This book would not be possible without the marvelous contributions by all "The Ladies of Leavenworth." I wish to thank you for your courage to leap into uncharted literary territories and for sharing your truths with me.

To Marlene Sider, my best friend, who has followed the evolution of this book from its earliest stages. This book would not have been written without your support and encouragement. Your steadfast belief in me never waivers, and your friendship will always be my beacon of light.

I wish to thank Paul Geffner, who gave me the opportunity to write this book in Paradise.

To Vicki Noble, I am grateful for your deep understanding of the feminine psyche and soul. You have provided me with keen insights and helped me to restore my faith.

To my parents, Sid and Toby, I thank you for your love and your emotional support through my difficult passages.

MaryEllen, you are a sweetheart. I am indebted to you for transforming what could have been an arduous process into one of ease.

Ellen Cole and Esther Rothblum, you have made publishing this book a delightful process. I am pleased to have worked with you on this project and appreciate your recognition of the importance of women's words.

And from dream to dream you wake up more and more conscious, more and more woman. The more you let yourself dream, the more you let yourself be worked through, the more you let yourself be disturbed, pursued, threatened, loved, the more you write, the more you escape the censor, the more and more woman in you is affirmed, discovered and invented.

–Hĕlĕne Cixous, *Coming to Writing and Other Essays,*
Edited by Deborah Jenson (Boston, Massachusetts,
Harvard University Press, 1991, pg. 55).

Chapter One

The Process of Writing

Everyone has a story to tell and a unique way to tell that story. No matter what age you are, what financial status you attain, what ethnic background you have, or what geographical location you live in, your life is indelibly inked with your own special stamp. Your life is peopled with a host of characters who gave to you, took from you, enchanted you, seduced you, and helped fashion the one-of-a-kind individual that you are. That self is always in a state of flux as you meet the joys and the challenges inherent in your path. Writing is one of the most powerful vehicles for self-discovery, understanding, and healing. I believe that writing one's life not only serves as a personal guide to understanding one's past, but frequently can point the way to one's future.

Writing has always been my obsession. Tracing my first scribblings in my diary when I was ten, I felt the urge to write early in my life. Like other children my age, I needed a special place, a companion, a trusted friend. My diary provided me with a safe place to record my fears, joys, hopes, and frustrations.

I was puzzled as a child and often scared. The silences in my home were deafening and I needed a place to explore my voice, to hear it, clearly and soundly. I never felt the need to defend myself, explain or question any of my written words, no matter how outrageous or indelicate. I believe that, even as a child, I inherently knew that writing was an act of alchemy. My writing served as a strong container, a holding ground, a safe haven. I could transform my anger, frustration, and loneliness onto the page. It was a potent and powerful act.

In my chaotic world, writing provided me with a great deal of clarity and understanding. I never felt truly connected with the world, and my writing offered me a chance to embark on an exciting journey. I could travel freely in my imaginative world and transform my boredom and malaise into creativity.

Even now, almost 30 years later, when I read the large hand-scrolled words in my diary, I have the opportunity to connect with that little girl. I would write quickly, a habit I still embrace; and the words in my diary ring strangely familiar today.

My writing voice, the voice that lives inside me, has always been insistent. Those commanding whispers have been with me since childhood. When I choose to listen to those voices, I experience the magic that is writing.

The writing process carried within it a unique blend of enchantment. Although I used to believe that I was the author charting my journey on the blank page, I now know otherwise. The writing takes me. As the words reveal themselves to me on paper, I am progressively led into each new sentence and paragraph. I love the process of writing.

I believe that everyone has her own voice to guide her writing life. Developing one's voice, whether it is through writing or another creative medium, is transformative. Yet, unless we stop to listen, to allow those voices to address us, we will never truly write in a veritable manner.

This book is a guide to writing about important experiences in your own life with authenticity, vitality, humor, and compassion. This book is different than other books of its genre since this book is written as a guide to both a woman's external and internal autobiographical experiences.

This is not a book about how women's lives have been devalued and deprived. This is not a book about what should have been. It is a book about what can be.

While you read this book, I would like you to think of me as your guide. In your writing journey, I wish you joy, success, pride, and a sense of accomplishment in your work. Indeed, everyone does have a story to tell and yours need not wait any longer.

A hush comes over the writing, an emotion akin to awe: so, something just beyond my own intelligence seemed to whisper when I began writing about my grandmother's garden which I couldn't imagine anyone caring about, it isn't a matter of whether you *can* go home again. You just do. Language, that most ghostly kind of travel, hands out the tickets. It never occurred to me, once given my ticket, to refuse it.

–Patricia Hampl, "The Need to Say It,"
from *The Writer On Her Work, Volume II,*
New Essays in New Territory
Edited by Janet Sternburg (W.W. Norton
and Company, Inc., 1991, pg. 26).

Chapter Two

In the Habit of Writing

Usually, getting started is the most difficult step to take in any creative venture and yet it is one of the most important moments. I strongly suggest that before you begin, you make some important commitments to yourself. You may choose to write by yourself, or you may want to work with friends who are of like mind. A common problem for women is that they do not value their creative lives and find excuses not to commit to their work. But remember, there will always be the laundry, the children, the dinners, the unfinished tasks from the office, and other responsibilities.

I have discovered a truth: *there is never enough time.* It doesn't matter. What matters most is that you find a time period when you commit to your writing. This time is your own and must be honored. I suggest that you set aside two hours a week for your writing. It doesn't matter when, just that you do it. If you find that you have more time, so much the better; but, start with two hours a week, and add more time as your spirit moves you.

Take out your calendar and look it over. Find two hours in the next week when you can write. Don't sandwich it in when you are doing errands, working on a project, or waiting to pick up your children from school. Find two hours of uninterrupted time. *Write down your name in pen* next to the hours that you have selected on your calendar. You may want to write down this time slot for each week for the next few months. Remember, it doesn't matter if you work for two hours during the evening one week, and two hours on a Sunday morning; what matters is that your commitment begins *now*!

When you write, be mindful of times when you can concentrate. If you have an answering machine for your phone, put it on. If your husband, lover, or children are home during this time, tell them you are working and *are not* to be disturbed! Close the door, take out your pen and pad, or turn on your computer. Don't feel guilty. I guarantee that if you documented how many hours you spend in service to others, two hours a week would not seem very much time at all. Think of it as a time in service to you.

Another useful vehicle for reaffirming your agreement to yourself is to write out the following contract and keep it pinned to your refrigerator, your bulletin board, or carry it in your wallet. The following is an example, but feel free to create your own contract.

"I, (*your name here*), a writer, will spend two hours a week writing. I will commit to working from (*your time slot*) each (*day of week you have selected*) undisturbed. I will not take phone calls, clean the house, or be disturbed in any way."

Once you commit to your writing, you may find yourself scrupulously guarding and enjoying that time each week. Even if it is difficult in the beginning, and you feel frustrated with your writing, stick to your agreement with a strong resolve. Honoring your writing begins with honoring your commitment to yourself.

I would like to dispel one of the most prevalent myths about writing. Along with the notion that writers wear berets, smoke cigarettes, hang out in bars, and create "at will," it is the last idea which stops so many women writers. The idea that writers create perfect prose upon command is a myth. Some writers may have this ability, but I have yet to meet one. Writing requires attention, imagination, and possibility. When you write, invite your words to appear to you freely without censorship. You can worry later about grammar and punctuation. Writing perfect prose effortlessly does not usually occur for most writers. Give yourself permission *not* to be perfect. Trust that your writing will evolve, and the more time that you spend in the habit of writing, the more comfortable you will be.

Some of my students have told me that they love to write in a cafe. One woman in my writing group, Jyoti, would visit the same Russian Hill coffeehouse each Monday evening before class, hurriedly writing to meet the 7 p.m. class. She enjoyed her ritual, the writing under pressure, and the chance to write in a comforting environment.

You may want to write alone or with other women of like mind. Perhaps a friend, or woman writer in your neighborhood may wish to join you. It really doesn't matter with whom you write, what matters is that *you write.*

Where you write is important as well, but don't be discouraged if you do not possess "a room of your own." If you don't have an office or a room to write in exclusively, be creative. A kitchen or a dining room table, a treehouse in your backyard, an attic, or a table and chair in your garage or basement can all become your writing workshop. Don't let the lack of an office dissuade you from your work. Devotion to your writing should not hinge on the accoutrements of space. Your proper intention is all that is required of you.

Feel free to improvise on any and all of the directions presented in this book. If your words come out in prose, poetry, dialogue or stream-of-consciousness writing, that is fine.

If you find that you are having difficulties getting started writing, then acknowledge the difficulties on the page. Use all the opportunities to express yourself. Write down phrases, lists, ideas about significant events in your life that you want to write about. You may want to develop a file marked, "Ideas," which you can use as you continue.

Many of my ideas come to me at odd times, even when I am at exercise class or when I am taking a bath. *Write down your ideas when they first come to you!* If you don't take your ideas seriously, then your Muse may not revisit you. Keep a notebook by your bed, in your purse, and in your car so that, when your ideas arrive, you can jot them down. I can't tell you how many times I have lost beautiful prose because I was too lazy to write it down.

This book is written for you as a guide so that you can be led through the process of writing autobiography. This book does not resemble the how-to-write-autobiography books on the market because I didn't want to replicate that format. The ideas and the exercises in this book point the woman writer to pay attention to her internal and psychological process.

I wanted this book to be different, accessible, and inspirational. I wanted to reach women across the country who want to tell their stories but feel isolated, alone, and unsure how to begin. If you choose to work with another woman, or with a group of women, you will find that sharing your words is quite a powerful experience. At the end of the book, I have suggestions for books to read and contacts for writing organizations.

Please listen to this next piece of advice with great attention: *Do not show your writing to family members*! Many of my students have shown their work to controlling parents, domineering sisters, insensitive brothers, and sabotaging lovers. If you choose to do that, you may be setting yourself up for failure. Family and friends, though well-meaning, frequently want to change your prose so that it does not expose them in an unflattering manner. Sometimes, our partners don't understand what we are writing, and they may be afraid that they will be written about in less than complimentary ways.

If you want to show your work to anyone, choose a supportive writing partner or friend who will reserve judgement. There are over a million periodicals, journals, literary magazines and newspapers where your work can be published, so you may consider submitting it. Also, there are many women's magazines actively seeking women's words. It is important that women make responsible choices for their work and trust in that. Choose your critics wisely.

WRITING EXERCISE

Before you begin writing about your life, I would like you to think about how you feel about writing. We all have our personal mythology of what a writer is and does. I would like you to write for fifteen minutes to complete the following sentence: *A writer is someone who_____.*

Write for fifteen minutes without stopping, letting yourself explore the possibilities. Let go of all your inhibitions and enjoy yourself. Remember to be honest. When you are finished, take a look at what you have written. Did anything surprise you?

If you are working with a partner, take turns reading what each of you has written and discuss the work.

Now, I would like you to complete the following sentence which will offer valuable insights as to your beliefs about yourself as a writer: *I want to write about my life but _____ stops me.*

Write for fifteen minutes without editing yourself. See what comes up for you. Remember, you can trust the writing. *It is the truth. Your truth.* When you read your work, pay attention to what ideas you have about what blocks you in your writing, and think about ways in which you can discard those blocks in a creative manner. Use your writing to understand and exorcise your own demons–don't let it use you.

I urge my students, when they feel blocked or can't seem to get started in their writing, to take out a piece of paper and "write" the block out, literally. For example: "I am so blocked in this work, I don't want to write, I am too busy, I have other things to do. I have responsibilities and this is just a hobby." Just write whatever it is you are feeling; be truthful, and if you are patient and honest, you can extricate yourself from obstacles by this process.

Throughout this book, I am including pieces that were written by the women in my autobiography classes. I have edited the work for length when necessary, but I have tried to adhere to the original form and style in which it was written. Some of the work is in prose, poetry, or stream-of-consciousness writing. Choose whatever form you feel comfortable with.

The following writing pieces address blocks in writing that occur for many women. Notice the difference in style, form, and language.

WHERE DOES MY WRITING PASSION LIE?

I rarely get headaches, but the notion of unleashing my passion brings on one; or, is it the caffeine? Fred used to say that everything is done out of love or fear.

–Cary Davis

My lovers insist on unveiling my writing so they can say, "Is this supposed to be part of something? Your ideas aren't very coherent, but you've got something here. Maybe you will be a writer some day if you work at it."

–Sandra Stevens

The silence within is like a pain. It is a quiet sadness that is loud and insistent. It is black and it is forever. I must have been born with it because I don't know where it comes from, where it begins. They have seen the real me and have guessed my secret.

–Rebecca Geiger

My voice is weak, scratchy and faint like the first sound I try to make upon awakening. Can I become an ally to the voice that yearns so much to become a presence? Can I give it a surprise party with gifts of time and sharp pencils? Can I welcome it out of the tiny shell into the glowing light of the clearing?

–Kathleen Byrne

The silent voice inside of me is reluctant to speak up. Mostly because none of them have exposed themselves that way. They all have more voices than I, even more silent voice.

–Jeanne Dorward

I've been silent so long I've forgotten the language. Sh, sh, sh, someone will hear. Held back, muffled. It only comes out through a knothole distorted–it has lost its life. What was young and full and new is withered, old and tired of waiting.

–Jyoti Haney

Chapter Three

A Room of One's Own

When Virginia Woolf addressed the Art Society at Girton in October 1928, little did she know that her essay, "A Room of One's Own," would become one of the most famous feminist essays of our time. She would be pleased to know that more women are taking out their pens to embrace their creativity with abandon; and, saddened that they still doubt their abilities and their "right to write." Unlike Ms. Woolf, we are fortunate to have access to the libraries and to study and purchase books; yet many of us are still imprisoned in our minds.

Ms. Woolf argues magnificently for a woman's need to have a room of her own and some money to go with it. I could not adequately explain her points as articulately as she, nor would I want to. In my work, I frequently use her model of a "room of one's own" and would like to share it with you.

A figurative "room of one's own" speaks to us in greater depth than a literal room. It is a place to feel safe in, a mindset of comfort, a blanket of support whether real or imagined. Many of the women writers who write about their rooms have revisited rooms of pleasure, rooms of love, rooms with faint smells of just-baked bread, steaming hot cups of cocoa and fresh cookies from childhood. Many times, these rooms do not literally exist for us in our lifetime, but exist in our mind's eye as a source of solace. In these rooms, our souls reside.

Some women choose to remember rooms filled with the musty odors of another time and place. Other women write about rooms where they felt safe and protected. It doesn't matter what rooms you remember or wish to write about. What matters is that you write about some room in your life, real or imaginary, that is important to you.

DIRECTIONS

Take a moment and make yourself comfortable. Close your eyes, uncross your legs, and take some deep breaths. As you exhale, gently listen to your breath and concentrate on nothing. Keep breathing. After a few moments, imagine that you are visiting a room of great importance in your life. This room may be real or imagined. It may be a room that you have spent hours in, or years in, or you may have spent a fleeting afternoon there while on vacation. The choice is up to you.

Imagine that your third eye (the space between your two eyes, above the bridge of your nose) has a film camera in it. Run the camera in your mind's eye, taking in all that you can remember about this room. Put yourself in the room and pay attention to everything. See the room, smell the aromas it offers to you, notice the curtains, the time of year, how old you are. Listen to any noises that you hear and hear them for the first time. What do you see? What do you hear? What do you notice? How do you feel in this room? Take as long as you like.

When you are ready to depart from the room, quickly open your eyes and write down everything you can recall about this particular room. Don't worry about putting down the information in prose style, just make a list. Know that you will remember everything about the room that you need to. You may be surprised by the length of the list. One of my students wrote about a room in her grandmother's house that she hadn't visited since she was a very small girl. She recalled the tiny photograph of her grandfather in the corner of the bedroom, the damp smell of his boots on the carpet, and her grandmother's distinctive perfume. When you can train yourself to see everything through a camera lens, you are better able to capture the moment without distractions. It is a wonderful method to embrace in your daily life.

After you have finished writing down your list, I would like you to draw a picture of the room. Don't worry if you aren't an artist. This is not an art assignment. When you write about this room, you will use the drawing as a roadmap to guide you in your prose. Take a few moments and, when you are ready, put the drawing in front of you. If you are working with other women, introduce the room to them and explain what captured your attention in the room and why this room was important to you.

After you have the drawing in front of you, write for twenty minutes as much as you can recall about the room. Don't worry about style, length, grammar, or structure. You needn't write for anyone else, just write to please yourself. That is most important.

When I revisited a "room of my own," I wrote about the tiny sewing room in my Grandmother Roseman's home in Connecticut. It was my favorite room in her huge house because it was *her* room. This was the room where she spent most of her time, sewing and dreaming. It was filled with threaded spools of every color which invited my small fingers to play with them. Her Singer machine, circa 1920, was propelled by her feet, and she used to let me sit on her lap while she hit the pedals since my short baby legs couldn't reach. The room smelled like her, a mixture of salt and baking powder. She always smelled like she was fresh from the oven herself.

In this room, I was free to touch anything I liked for as long as I liked. While the other members in my family visited my grandfather, uncle, and grandmother downstairs, I would spend hours upstairs touching the beautifully textured remnants of materials she had clumped into a basket. I have her sewing machine and frequently press my palm softly upon it, close my eyes, and remember her.

The following examples of writing are varied, rich in texture and design. They illustrate the wide tapestry of experiences from various women's lives.

WOMEN'S VOICES

Muted colors, green, rose, golden yellow. The smell of cigars, horehound drops, whatever flowers were arranged on the marble table, Grandpa's after-shave. The cool green air of the screen porch wafting in with outside sounds on its hem.

Two secretaries, like mahogany skyscrapers at either side of the screen porch door, ceramic birds behind the glass panes, nestled in the nooks left by small books. Blue and white import-ware teapots line the mantle. Polished-patina, brass spark screen and fire tools leaning, waiting to be called into service for the odd poke or prod.

Along one wall, under the moonlit ocean oil painting, is the divan (as Grams calls it) like a resting camel, begging to be bounced upon. Faded orientals ripple on the floor, atop the rose-colored carpet.

My favorite things in this welcoming room inhabit a warm pool of memory. My Grandpa would come home from the bank and give his "Onion" a hug. He would lift me up, ("Elliot, you're back."–I can hear Gram) and ask me if I wanted to hear his birdie sing. "He's sleeping now, but he'll wake up for us." He would take the brass birdcage from the top bookshelf and wind and wind the key. A green enamel bird chirped on command, singing a long tune. For years, I thought that if I turned around quick enough or was quiet enough, I would catch the birdie in some act of life. Never happened but I kept trying.

On the porch was a three-story dollhouse complete with glass in the windows, a porch light, silver service and a porcelain-headed family. Friends of my grandparents owned a toystore and generously gifted the grandparents of four granddaughters. Many hours of bickering ensued, and I felt I was in heaven when I had the dollhouse to myself.

My favorite spot in the room was my Grandpa's big yellow chair. Overstuffed, round and welcoming, sort of like Grandpa, the chair was imbued with his cigar smoke and aftershave. The standing ashtray next to it usually held a half-smoked cigar and any cigar rings acquired during the week. He saved those for his "girls" and I felt honored when he slipped one on my finger.

My Grandpa died when I was still a little girl. For years his chair was left, virtually untouched except for dusting, as a sort of monument. I would sit in it when I visited my grandmother and breathe deeply to capture a remnant of his aroma, but it was gone.

–Nancy Wilson

*   *   *

It is September in a different country. We sit outside in the garden. The windows of a small hotel are all open and the pieces of conversation float above our heads. The sun has slipped behind the trees but it is still too early for dinner. Below us and to the right are the vineyards. A man standing in the vineyard waves to another and walks away. The garden is small and filled with heather, lavender, and jasmine. In some places the dirt is damp and there are footprints in the ground. We open a bottle of wine. The cork rolls across the little table. Inside the hotel, plates and glasses are carried from the kitchen to the dining room. A waiter moves from table to table with silverware and white napkins. We toast one another and the disappearing sun.

–Joyce Roschinger

* * *

I guide the borrowed Alpha Romeo to a stop against the curb, wondering if Kathleen is home so I can collect my mail at this soon-to-be new address. They have started painting the outside of the cottages–a deep dark brick red with white trim around the windows and doors. The old broken picket fence has been removed.

My feet crunch across the gravel driveway. As I step up to the front porch of Kathleen's cottage, I imagine her having some comments about the work not being done to her liking, but a knock on the door is answered by silence. Hoping she'll return, I walk around the side of the back garden and my cottage. The garden is piled high with boxes, paint cans, old shelves from the inside walls, ivy vines that had been torn away from the outside walls. Bushes that had been growing beneath the front windows have been pulled out by the roots, their leaves beginning to wither.

I look through the pane windows to the fresh, clean, only room of my cottage, all bright and white, awaiting me like a newly stretched canvas. It seems to be asking me: "What colors will you choose for this painting of your new life?" The answer is part scared, part excited feeling. There is nothing of the familiar here; no cozy place of refuge. It is daunting, yet inviting me to be as new and fresh as the white walls.

–Jyoti Haney

* * *

Prologue

The box does not exist for me any longer–only in the deepest recesses. I cannot believe I allowed myself to be subjected to the fears for so long.

The Story

The room is white and expansive–the sun pours into the room from the window–the window is high on the wall. White curtains of sheer cotton move from the gentle breeze. The white of the room reflects the shadows and the very whiteness of itself–white, white, white, blinding, clean, and free.

The wood floor has been scraped and stained white so it is barely wood-like, the grain just visible.

There is no door.

(One wonders who places everything in this room.)

The rocking horse is life-size, made of walnut. His name is carved in a realistic style.

There is a wicker chair. It is also painted white. It is large and comfortable.

There is nothing else in this room. How did I get in here, I think.

Mounting the horse so high off the ground requires help from a step stool that is nearby. I feel very high up–and a little frightened. But the rocking horse feels safe under me. The wood is warm and smooth. I keep running my hands over his head and along his body. At first I am still. Soon the movement of the horse sets up a rhythm that captivates me. I laugh and feel joyous. I feel so good. I never want to get off. I am at once a child and a grown-up. I can ride forever.

–Rhoda London

*   *   *

In the clear mountain air, the tinkling sounds of the cowbell are like wind chimes. Gentle, melodious, they calm the listener. Unseen, they might be the footsteps of angels, dancing in unison.

The reality is these are cowbells, draped about the necks of beasts weighing hundreds of pounds. Cows are not known for their grace, for their fairy-tale movements; but here, it seems they tread lightly, so delicately that they seem ethereal.

From the hotel room, the sound wafts through the open window. In the distance, the flowering apple tree's blossoms flutter slowly in the gentle breeze. The bells are the soundtrack of the soul.

Even when the cows move into view, this image is not dispelled. There are no herds, plodding and jostling, with their bells clanking and clanging. Somehow, there is harmony.

Perhaps if I were a musician, I could tell you what chord they play. Someone very wise selected the tone of these bells. It's loud enough to let the owner know where the animal is and what direction it might be moving, yet soft enough not to be a disruption, an interruption or an annoyance. And somehow, too, it seems to soothe the wearer.

This sound is soothing to the human ear as well. In the evening, it's a lullaby that rocks me to sleep. In the morning, it's the gentlest of sounds to awaken me. The tinkling caresses my ears like a tropical night caresses my skin. It's so serene that it seems impossible that anyone, anywhere, could be other than caring, loving, and assured of the goodness of man. I am in love with the world.

The great natural beauty of the setting is undeniable. The mountains, the fields, the orchards, the lake–all are set perfectly and exquisitely. The melody playing touches a chord within me, enhancing the experience immeasurably.

–Jeanne Dorward

* * *

It was a long time ago. A very long time ago. A time when I would skip up and down the sidewalk of Gladstone Street and between the parts of the skip, when my feet would touch the pebbly pavement, I would fly high into the smoky Pittsburgh air. I could feel the sullen summer breeze in my straight short hair and I was soaring!

My laughter tears from my gap-toothed mouth as I fly up and landed down in a wonderful rhythm. I would skip and fly, skip and fly until I was sweaty and out of breath and then crawl beneath the green hedge that surrounded the house and the yard. I would spy on the ants and the crickets with their huge jointed legs and jagged jaws. I could turn the hollyhock blossoms into pink ballerinas and make them dance to my symphony of hums.

I could pick a handful of tart green gooseberries from the prickly bush in Grandpa's yard and squash them together with a big silver spoonful of sugar and taste the magic of a green and white pie. Mrs. Banya's mulberry tree had berries that tasted good whether they were hard and green, crunchy and pink or soft and dripping with the purple juice that she said made the silk so soft when the silkworms ate mulberry leaves in China.

The only silk I knew was in Mama's top drawer–a pale peach bedjacket with beige lace and a black knitted snood with tiny pearls sewn in the corners of the triangles. Did this old crooked lady ever wear this mysterious headdress? Did her perfume in the heavy bottle smell so strong and sharp that Grandpap could still smell it through his nose that had stopped working? I could check into the depths of the blue vase that perched on the rickety hall table and sort and re-sort the treasures inside; rubber bands, hair pins, butter-rum Lifesavers, a rusty hook that she said was for buttoning shoes when she was little, one rhinestone earring, a ticket stub for a trainride, a stamp with German words on it.

I could look at the beautiful patterns on the pink and green wallpaper–a pink stripe behind the most beautiful feathery ferns–the patterns could change and get stranger if I carefully peeled some of the pink background away.

In the winter I could look through the jagged ice castles on the hall window that looked across into Mrs. Crawford's upstairs and see her tiny hunched shape walk slowly down the long hallway–a dark witch in her icy lair. On cold Saturday mornings I burrowed into the vastness of the brown satin quilt on our bed. When the furnace finally sent up some heat it was time to venture out and start the winter games. My sister and I sent slender bobbypin toboggans down steep and dangerous pillowcase ravines. The Indian girl in the porcelain sari and the Hawaiian girl in the china grass skirt and lei never seemed to mind the cold and went gladly sliding down the hills again and again when their turns came.

Our dolls would leap out the windows into snowbanks two stories below and be saved in shoebox ambulances that screamed down the stairway in reckless rescues of the horribly bloodied Betsy and Ree-Ree.

We sneak scarves, bathrobes, and handkerchiefs from the closet in my parents' neat quiet bedroom and put them around our heads and necks and chests and find the album with the veiled dancing girls on the cover and turn on the hi-fi-*loud*. We whirl madly around the vast marble coolness of the Arabian Nights living room, with its velvet chaises and carved coffee tables suddenly studded with jewels and tiny mirrors. My silken turban would barely stay on my head through the dizzying turns I would make to the spiraling music of *Scheherazade*.

At night I would travel on the voice of my mother to the dark woods and feel the terrible sadness of Bambi and his brave mother. Her goodnight would echo through the moonlit birch trees where the silent owls and snowshoe rabbits lived. And soon I would lie back on my cool floating pillow and feel the vastness of space and wonder about the planets and feel the breeze of infinity touch my face between the warm rhythm of my little sister's sweet breath.

–Kathleen Byrne

Chapter Four

Creating Personal Power Shields

I have always secretly wished that I was an artist, able to paint a visual recording of images which could and would mirror my inner world accurately. Unfortunately, I did not inherit my mother's artistic ability. While I was studying for my Master's Degree in Dance Therapy at Lesley College in Cambridge, I had the opportunity to explore the multi-uses of art as a therapeutic means. I was amazed to discover how powerful the process of creating art is, and I found it particularly appealing to work with people who did not consider themselves artists, perhaps because I was of the same ilk.

I decided to incorporate the use of art in tandem with my writing groups because I found it one of the best vehicles for recording information honestly. Frequently, when writers write, they censor themselves by listening to that infamous saboteur, "the critic." When you are asked to draw, and draw quickly, that inner critic does not have time to manifest and cannot stop you. The use of drawing in tandem with guided visualizations helps you access information accurately and without any interference.

Usually, in my writing sessions, I guide the women writers through visualizations concerning some aspects of their lives. I urge them to recall the images, colors, and textures that arise from the visualizations. Often, writers report hearing lines of prose or just one important word. Other writers may see a color, a potent image or a texture. Remember, that it doesn't matter what you see, hear, or experience, for whatever you decide to draw or to document on paper will be right for you.

Sometimes the drawing may prompt, aid, confuse, or even surprise you. It is not necessary to understand and decipher the meaning. All that is needed is an open mind and a willingness to record what occurs. Think of yourself as a reporter, merely documenting what you see, hear, or intuit.

Don't worry if you don't consider yourself an "artist." It really doesn't matter whether you are able to draw in a sophisticated or even elementary manner. Just record everything you experience as your truth on paper.

For those of you who don't "see" anything, don't worry. I never see images when I am doing any type of visualization. Instead, I "hear" a line or a word that speaks directly to me. Remember that each woman's experience is authentic for her and that there is no prescribed form to follow.

CREATING PERSONAL POWER SHIELDS

A Power Shield documents your life's experiences in a manner that is deceptively simple. The shield is a circle that you create, filled with images, words, or symbols that you choose to document your past, present, and future. It's a lovely visual representation of your struggles and triumphs in your life so far.

The idea for a Power Shield is not a new one and is frequently used by therapists as a vehicle for documenting important times in your life; psychologically and literally. (The exercise that I have used in this chapter is adapted from the book, *Personal Mythology, The Psychology of Your Evolving Self*, David Feinstein and Stanley Krippner, PhD (Jeremy Tarcher Inc., Los Angeles, page 33.)

The visual images in this shield portend the invisible worlds. I liken them to the lovely images of Indian Healing Shields made by the Medicine Women of the tribe. These Power Shields offer the woman writer an individualized spectrum of healing images to work with.

It is my hope that when each woman writer places her Power Shield in front of her, she will have a visual documentation of her life so far, a record of her life to date, knowing that she alone has the power to change her next steps in life, at will. The accompanying prose, or "words of power," for each exercise, can provide a wealth of writing material to use when examining a woman's life. Your life.

Traditionally, the shield has been used as armor to fend off enemies, attract suitors, and protect its wearer. The power inherent in this shield exists simply because it is self-designed. It is yours. Its strength reflects your strength; its sorrow mirrors your sorrow; and its joy celebrates with you.

During some of my workshops, the women writers have created gorgeous and colorful Power Shields from pen and ink, colored pens, magic markers, and crayons. You may want to add particular talismans to your shield as you create it; photographs, feathers, ribbons, buttons, or other objects of meaning to you. Before you begin the Power Shield exercises, be prepared with all the necessary articles. You will need a large sheet of white paper and some colored pens to begin.

This exercise takes time and I urge you to work on one section during each writing session. It doesn't matter if you don't finish the shield in one day. What matters is that you complete the exercise during the next few weeks.

If you choose to work with another woman on these exercises, you may want to take turns reading the directions aloud to each other. If you are working alone, you may want to use a tape recorder and record the directions for all of the writing exercises in this book.

DIRECTIONS FOR PART I: PARADISE LOST

Draw a large circle on the paper. Divide the circle into four quadrants and label them on the outside of the circumference of the circle; Paradise Lost, Paradise, My Quest, and, My Writing Muse. Set your circle aside and close your eyes.

I want you to imagine that you are visiting a place in your life called Paradise Lost. I want you to recall, not relive, a time in your life when everything seemed lost to you. This may be a time of upheaval, a time of personal or financial struggle, or a time of confusion. *Every woman* has experienced a descent to Paradise Lost, so don't be reluctant. Remember that you are safe during your visit. I don't want you to relive the feelings, but simply document that time. You don't need to actively access the pain and defeat you felt at that time. Think of yourself as a reporter gathering the facts and taking down the notes without personal involvement.

Remind yourself, if you are experiencing discomfort, that you ultimately prevailed and rose above those dark days. If you are currently experiencing a period of pain, know that you have all of the necessary resources and strengths close at hand to clear your head. Allow your writing to lead you out of the darkness so you can make the best decisions for yourself.

When you are finished thinking about Paradise Lost, take a moment to breathe deeply. I want you to release these images, totally knowing that they cannot keep you in this dark, difficult place. Introduce a peaceful symbol, a loving symbol, a symbol of balance before you and open your eyes. Take a few minutes to regain your balance.

Now, I would like you to take your crayons or colored pens and draw the images that presented themselves to you during the visualization. Don't worry what it looks like. It is not necessary to understand the images. If you only saw a color, then put that color on the shield. If you didn't see anything, but heard a word, then write that word in the Paradise Lost quadrant of the circle. What matters in this exercise, as well as the others in this book, is that you only draw what is real and true for you during the visualization. Don't change the image in any way.

Take twenty minutes and write down quickly, without editing, what "Paradise Lost" means to you. If you want to begin by describing the image, that is fine. If it is helpful for you to begin with, "My Paradise Lost looked like _____ ," use that example.

When you are done, I want you to read your piece aloud, regardless of whether you are working solo or with another woman. A very important component of the writing process is the reading of the work. The spoken word can have as much impact as the written word. I believe that the reading, the affirmation of, and the sounds of the language, unleash your writing power. Resist any impulse to make judgments about the work or to solve any problems in the content of the material.

WOMEN'S VOICES

Paradise was lost to me when I became distracted by conflict and loss. No mother, no father . . . those erratic, powerful, self-absorbed gods couldn't see me. I was put into the hands of people who did not care for who I really was and who even hurt me. I became unseen, void, empty-hearted . . . because *I* was not good enough. Without warning, nor understanding why, I was left unsupported. The bad girl was abandoned, denied warmth, comfort, connection and nurture. She was left full of rage and pain, unplugged. For so long, I lost myself and feared others. Who or what could I trust?

–Paula Denman

*   *   *

I miss us immensely. Not all the time. But at different times. Before I fall asleep. Or when I have had a particularly difficult day. And especially when I have done something fine in my life. It is many years later after that excursion to the wine country. Our friends are no longer married. They got a divorce in our sixth year of marriage. She is now married to a younger man, five years younger with a boyish smile. He wants children. She does not. She still wears her unusual earrings and laughs that great laugh. But I don't see her as often. My husband's friend has lived in different places with different women. I have not been able to tell if women leave him or he leaves women. He sends us postcards every time he moves. No date on the card, only the postmark. No salutation. Only the words, "I've moved." I miss us immensely.

–Joyce Roschinger

*   *   *

I dreamed of angels
When you died.
All were women in
Long white dresses.
They cradled you now
And floated along
Feet above the ground
To show me you.
I could see only,
But not touch
Your radiant beauty

Of another world.
White-gold and soft
In their arms,
Secure, loved and safe
I knew . . . yet
My tears ran away
To hold you.

–Zoe Smith

* * *

The image of an early fetus, pink, soft, lonely, black eyes, the cord attached to the mother . . . me. The black tears . . . thousands of them. I wonder what it would have been like if I hadn't had the abortion. It was easy to get rid of you. The doctors made the decision for me. "This wouldn't be a healthy baby," they'd said. "After all the X rays and medication you've had, we recommend a therapeutic abortion."

So there it was–my solution to my problem. Little did I know that in ridding myself of you, you became a part of me forever. Your memory haunts me, years later. I've punished myself for making this mistake over and over.

First, I stopped caring about myself and let myself get mixed up with all the wrong men. One of them turned out to be a rapist. This was my biggest punishment of all–aside from the abortion. And to think it all happened that same year when I was just 21 years old. I still wonder if I will ever see you again. I still can't decide if I'm worthy of becoming a parent, me, a murderer!

–Mary Ellen Rescigno

DIRECTIONS FOR PART II: PARADISE

Close your eyes and think about a time in your life when you truly felt as if you were visiting Paradise. Paradise can be represented by a literal place, a person, or a moment in time. Only pleasant and positive sensations fill you. See all of the colors, symbols and textures of Paradise in your life. There will be a symbol, a color, or a sacred word waiting for you. Wait for the message to present itself to you; don't force it. Always honor your first thought or image.

When you are ready, take a moment and breathe in your color, image, word, or symbol. When you are finished, draw what you experienced under the heading, "Paradise."

After that, write for twenty minutes without editing your prose, about what Paradise meant to you. Let the pen lead you and trust that it will tell you all you are seeking. When you are finished, read your work aloud whether you are working alone or with others. Listen to your work; listen to your words with respect. What is missing from your prose? What did you especially enjoy writing? What would you like to hear more of?

Now that your shield is half-finished, you may see a direct parallel between Paradise Lost and Paradise, but this needn't be the case for everyone. If you have the time and the inclination, I would like you to spend some time writing about the half-finished shield and the relationship between Paradise and Paradise Lost.

*   *   *

WOMEN'S VOICES

A clear, warm day with touches of spring in the air. There are four of us in the white Volkswagen. We drive with the top down. Two men and two women, two sets of married people. On the way to have Sunday brunch in the wine country. The men sit in the front and we sit in the back. Everything smells clean, fresh, new. We talk about what we have done this week, our jobs. One of the men in the front seat is my husband. We have been married only a short time. The other man who is driving is his best friend. They talk, they laugh. Their conversation is loud, exciting, rising above the car. They are both tall, handsome men with flecks of gray in their hair already. Looking at the back of their heads, I love them immensely. I sit next to my friend. She wears unusual earrings. I like the way she laughs. As if she had just discovered how to laugh. Sometimes we include the men in our conversation. We are on our way to have brunch at a winery. I have looked forward to this all week. We are young, newly marrieds riding in a car with the top down. The air is fresh, the day so clear that it hurts my eyes.

–Joyce Roschinger

*   *   *

Whispers . . . the sounds vibrate in my bones. When the wind catches in the branches of trees, I'm suddenly silenced. I wait and listen. It's the voices of the Higher Spheres speaking to me. And these are the only sounds: the breeze in the trees and my heart beating in my ears. A warm breeze pushes against my skin; caresses me. Vibrates my still body to the roots. What's dead and loose in me shakes to the ground. And fruits fall. I'm left without need or desire and feel full of love. Full of the easy flow of life, internally peaceful, trusting, nurtured. Feeling connected, in unity. *That* is paradise. No conflict within. Paradise is in my heart; not far away at all.

–Paula Denman

*   *   *

The image of light, diffused color, a host with the cross, peacefulness, safety, forgiveness–humility, cleansing, tears. I came to the priest on a weekend retreat, five years later, to confess what I had done–to ask someone, anyone, to forgive me! The priest couldn't see my face, so it was easier, but I was sure he knew my voice. It didn't matter. He was there to absorb my pain.

After confessions were heard, I saw him leave the brown wooden box, all pale and hunched over, looking extremely sad and tired. He was a very young man, tall, lanky, with stringy blond hair and long arms that hung at his sides. He felt all the pain that I had felt.

I told him about the abortion. I told him I wasn't worthy to become a mother. He said, "You've suffered a lot–You realize it was a mistake–You are forgiven. . . . Go, and sin no more." Sitting in church, I felt peaceful and relieved for the first time in many years.

The times I have received communion, the thin wafer on my tongue, I have felt quite humble. I have also felt like crying, and sometimes I do. The tears just flow and even though my mind feels clear and I can't speak, I feel the tears cleansing me, rolling down my cheeks. I feel loved, protected, happy.

I've stayed away now for over a year. I have been struggling and yet, I haven't gone back to the place that helps me feel forgiven and new. I want to find this place inside myself, but I'm not sure how. I wonder if it's possible to do this without turning to someone else, or sitting inside a church. It would be nice if I could find paradise inside myself.

Maybe paradise is the baby I never had, waiting to be born.

–Mary Ellen Rescigno

* * *

DIRECTIONS

Take out your shield and look at it. You should have the areas of Paradise and Paradise Lost filled in with your images as well as accompanying prose. Now, I would like you to turn your attention to the area of the circle marked, "My Quest." Close your eyes and think about your quest at this important time in your life. Think of yourself as a woman warrior on the road, creating your journey through your life. What is your goal? What is it that you are seeking? What do you look like? Where are you going?

Don't rush the images; let them unfold. You can trust that you are being presented with the truth, your truth. When you are ready, draw in the images on your shield or the words, symbols, or colors that are important for you to remember.

Then, put the shield in front of you and write for twenty minutes about what your quest means to you. Don't stop to edit your writing, just let the pen guide you. You can trust this process.

* * *

WOMEN'S VOICES

A sheet of paper to fill with words. I find a place of contentment when I write. The more often I write, the better I feel. Writing helps me understand events. Makes some sense and order out of living. I am able to see things from all angles. Sometimes what I write is painful, difficult to actually see on paper. But, not nearly as painful as when I carry it inside. I get a sense of power when I write. I keep hearing my father's words, "Stop trying to see because that's when you will start to really see things." Writing allows me to see. Memories of good days, wonderful relationships, painful situations all come together on paper. Different memories evoke different emotions which bring together various pieces of writing.

–Joyce Roschinger

*   *   *

So I think about my quest as a writer. It has something to do with solidifying a dream, giving form to an attitude of compassionate love through a word or phrase that grabs the heart and mind. It takes the breath, shakes you up, penetrates you, and infuses life into you. To inspire, to challenge, to have dialogue with the others; to teach by metaphor some solution, or give aid, or . . . what? To tell parables of individuals wrestling with themselves through internal change. All done with art and style. This art becomes a knife cutting through the dross, the useless fat, the lies . . . to reveal the meat, the gold; to adorn lives with hope and love, like a torch which throws light into the dark corners. I want to create words and pictures that shine like beacon lights in the night fog in order to mirror how we are and what we can become.

–Paula Denman

*   *   *

The message: "Put your horns away." . . . A little girl in a sparkly pink dress that flows. It touches the ground. She flies above me. I am lying on an ornate bed with lots of fluffy satin blankets and pillows. It is another time and place. I am not visible, except that I know that I have blonde hair. So does the little girl. She's like a guardian angel. I lay there sleeping peacefully. She flies over me and removes a pair of horns on a helmet, like a Viking would wear. She does this once and hides them behind a curtain so they are not visible. Another pair of horns appears on my head. She hurries over and removes them again.

The next scene is a brown wooden door, very worn, with dirty glass. There is a brown, long-handled broom. It is worn from much use. Someone pushes it through the glass. The glass shatters and flies all over the stairs and a white dove comes fluttering out of the door into the air. The gift: Peace.

–Mary Ellen Rescigno

* * *

In the following selections, the writers chose to write about all the components of the shield. Their work is a very creative integration of all of the elements of the shield. In total, the writing does indeed describe each woman's quest because it identifies key moments in her life.

Let me remind you that *there is no right way* to write these exercises. I invite you to let the words tell you what they want to tell you. Let the words lead you along your journey. Let the words dance on the page. When you stop your writing to engage in the "right" questions; "Is this right?" "Does this sound right?" and "Am I doing this right?" you stifle, choke, and drown your own words.

Every writer has her own form, her own rhythm, her own gift of language. I urge you to let your writer's voice develop and grow, always giving it room to adapt and change as you do.

WOMEN'S VOICES

I close my eyes to see paradise and immediately I am in the woods. I lie stretched out on a cool flat rock watching the babbling brook go by. The woods are dark and dense, the rock is cool, the water is happy and talkative. I am alone here–just me and nature and it feels fine. I can be sad, happy–whatever.

Suddenly, though from across the shore, a little creature comes hopping. He hops across the rocks which bridge the water and comes directly to me, nestling softly up beside me. It's a rabbit. I wish he were gray, or speckled, or something but he's not. He's a pure, white soft little rabbit.

When I close my eyes again, I am standing, the rabbit is in my arms, and we are at the edge of our pure and simple woods, stepping timidly across the border, entering a new wood–this one is very dark, very menacing. We stay in the corner, the far corner which borders our wood and this one. It's so dark, but we can see eyes–yellow, and orange cartoon eyes flash around us. The rabbit trembles in my arms and I press him to me, stroking his fur.

When I look up, I see the man. Or is it a shadow? He is all in black and his eyes flash, not only orange or yellow, but black. He takes just two steps from the trees and I know him too–there's something so very familiar that it's as if a force propels me to take a step forward. The rabbit jumps from my arms, and I walk toward the man turning to see the rabbit hopping back across the border.

I reach out for the man, and we move slowly toward each other, his eyes on my face, mine on his. On reaching mine, I see that he has the strength and the purpose of a knight. But when he locks me in his arms, I feel so frightened. Why do I stay? Because he has something to tell me. There's a reason he is here. We come closer and closer, and soon I see that he's not a knight at all, but an angel–a black angel. . . . I put my hand on his face, and stroke his beard. I close my eyes as I offer myself to him, thinking, "I'm so far away from home."

And, when I open my eyes again, I am in a wonderful clearing, wearing a long flowing dress. It's green with pretty yellow flowers, and feels light and cool against my skin. The woods surround me; the sky is blue; the birds are singing. There's a kitten in my lap and around me are goats and dogs. There are children who are my friends playing beside me. I feel something soft and warm brush my leg, and it's my rabbit friend acting as if I never left.

When it's time to go, we all leave at once–the animals, the children, the rabbit, and me. We find a spot, a perfect spot to build our home. Our house will be in a thick green wood, and our backyard will be a babbling brook.

–Rebecca Geiger

*   *   *

Paradise

Dear 9-year-old, tree-climbing, jacks playing, always in motion self,

Thank you for your adroitness, your spunk, your capability.

Through you, I recaptured courage, risk-taking, pursuit of goals that matter.

My skeleton remembers what you were,
how you stood, your life-force; I remember.

I'm jazzed.

Paradise Lost

Dear Me at 30,–Dear Me–,

I weep for your aloneness, for the intention-to-be-a-team-player–for having chosen the wrong partner. But most of all for being unequipped to see the-parallel-lives-you-two-will-always-experience and know that the kernel of the healing lies in the understanding of that.

But, now you don't know–there's not a glimmer of hope or help. Your marrow is squeezed dry, no juice, no breath, ugly, stupid, still.

I whisper to you–the lowest ebb is the turn of the tide.

My Guide Friday

Dear Friday, This is About You,

My Guide Friday is big and shaggy. I've seen him out the window of a plane headed for China, his ears whipping in the wind as he tore across the clouds to be with me there. When sick in Beijing, I pulled his soft fur around me and felt safe and comforted.

He is me and I am him. He is never far away, always a presence. He showed up in 1980 as I completed one life and began another. He's just what I've been needing to write my book.

Even though he's two stories high, I can lead him with a cobweb.

My Quest

Dear Me of Coming Year,

I will know you but you will wear a new skin–a southern seaside shimmery summer sky bodysuit.

Your journey will produce a book not without effort, but intrinsically.

And your name will have a different ring, a new tone closer to the one that resounds through your calls and your being. Sing on.

–Ruth Hynds

*   *   *

The last segment of the creation of your Power Shield is my favorite. This exercise entitled, "My Muse" or "My Guide" enables you to meet your Writing Muse, and/or your Writing Guide. Sometimes your Muse may appear in your visualization as a shadow, an insect, an animal; or, sometimes, people in your life who have died. Just pay attention during this exercise. Know that your Guide is there for you and you alone, not only in your writing life, but in your daily life.

I frequently call upon my Writing Muse when I am most in need of comfort and reassurance. My Muse is faceless, and her presence comes to me in whispers and tuggings on my left ear. She is the woman who whispers deep truths when I am most in need of hearing them. I listen intently, for I know that I can trust what she has to tell me, even if I don't necessarily want to pay attention.

I find it rather amusing that my Muse makes herself known by tugging on my ear. I think she is reminding me of my craving for solitude and the need to take more time for my work. Her tuggings insist that I pay attention and listen. Sometimes, I find myself in an internal argument about timing, but she always wins.

You may be surprised by the form or forms in which your Muse appears to you. One woman in my seminar was rather disappointed when she saw that her Muse was an old wrinkled elf of a man. She desperately wanted a frilly, ethereal goddess of writing to appear to her, but that was not what she received. I urged her to stay with the image, for she was chosen by this elf and, silly as it might sound, this elf belonged to her and vice versa.

During this exercise and the other exercises in the book, trust your first thought, for it is always correct. Try to avoid the urge to look for a preconceived image. Let it appear to you effortlessly.

DIRECTIONS

Close your eyes and think about your Muse or your Guide. What does it look like? What does it want to tell you? Know that this Muse only wants to help and support you. Just sink into a peaceful state and allow the image to surround you. When you are ready, open your eyes in the visualization, and pay attention. Expect that you will see someone, or something waiting for you. It may appear to you in a symbol, a color, an animal form, or even a mythological god. Keep an open mind.

Ask your Guide its name and listen to all it has to tell you. Thank your Guide for all its help and, if you have a particular question, or if you need help in a certain area in your life, say so. Be sure to ask how you can communicate with your Guide in your waking state, and how you can contact it when you are in need. Sometimes, your Guide has something to give you or to tell you. Just be aware of all that transpires between you.

When you feel sure that you will remember how to contact your Muse, open your eyes slowly. Take a few breaths. Now, draw the image of your Guide in a way that you will recognize. Don't worry how it looks, just try to put a symbol, a color, or even a word in the last quadrant of the circle. Sometimes, women writers (like myself) don't see anything. They only hear things. In that case, write down what you heard in the circle. If you "felt" something in particular in your body during the visualization, then document those feelings in your own way.

When you are ready, write for twenty minutes about this exercise. Write down all that you remember and don't worry about syntax. Read the prose aloud to your writing partner, and show the shield as well. If you are alone, read the prose aloud, and look at your Guide.

Your Muse can indeed surprise you. One of my students reported seeing her Guide as the mythological god, Mercury. He urged her to write and to believe in her writing. The verse she wrote that day was gorgeous; it was lyrical and very rhythmic. Yet, she doubted her abilities; and, even when her work was acknowledged and applauded that day, she dismissed her talents. This woman had an extraordinary gift for language, a gift she couldn't accept.

Now that your shield is finished, I want you to look at it. It clearly documents a woman's life, your life. I call it a Power Shield because of its essential power which cannot be dismissed. Frame your shield, carry it with you, post it in your office, and use it for actualizing your strength and talents.

The shield is your life *up to this moment*. It is a circle of information about where you came from, where you are headed; and with the added gift of your Guide, your have the supportive energy to get there. Your dreams may appear more vivid, and previously-closed doors of understanding in your life may open.

This Power Shield that you have created is a deceptively simple visual exercise. Your accompanying prose, or "words of power" are very potent. When you look at the prose that you have created for this exercise, you may be surprised by its depth. This information is not only richly inspirational, but healing. It is wise to take out your shield when you are doubting your talents in order to remind yourself of your special gifts.

WOMEN'S VOICES

My guide appeared to me in a meadow near Echo Lake. I lay on my back in the wildflowers smelling the pine trees and gazing at the blue sky dotted with a few white clouds floating away over the nearby mountain peaks.

As I lay in this meadow, at peace and totally unconcerned, I hear birds chirping and see an occasional one swooping then soaring aware somehow of movement near me. I look around and a beautiful doe came into view. She moves serenely and with majesty.

–Jeanne Dorward

*   *   *

A feisty gal guide
in a white canvas jump suit.
Swinging on a tarp rope
Swinging into unknown places.
Swinging between the dark and the light.

She has a mop of hair
and a big smile
and eyes that I trust
She warns me with sweetness
not to fear getting
trapped or entangled
in memories.
She reminds me of how
Chinese handcuffs work
When we pull back
Suddenly and with fear
We get stuck in the
tightening weave of straw
if we explore gently–
we are free to come and go.

–Kathleen Byrne

*   *   *

You've startled me swooping down so suddenly from that tall
lone pine. You fold in those magnificent wings, the feather tips
brush my bare arms. A shudder ripples across my back and down
my sides. I watch your talons curl around the wooden backrest of
this wooden bench.

There is only the sound now of the wind in
the pines–your feathers quiver. I lift my gaze to
finally meet your eyes
and see the deepest gentle welcoming there.
The stern eagle brows recede. I feel a deep question being
answered.
It is without words that I hear you speak to an
ancient longing. . . .

"I am here to guide you into the boundless unknown. I possess the
wisdom of the ages and I am here to help you remember who you
are; why you chose to come into the Earth.

I have been with you always, knowing precisely when this moment would arrive where you would allow the revelation of your true Being.

If you cast back, you will remember that crystal morning high in the Himalayas–the sun was just glistening off the highest snowy peak. I spoke through one of your companions, thus: 'On a day like this it's as if the whole world has just been born.' Tears of remembrance filled your eyes.

Now you may receive this gift and give birth to the world within so rich with the treasures of your living.

Know that I am always as close as your next breath. I am your inspiration. Together we soar to the highest peaks and plummet the deep canyons of creative expression."

–Jyoti Haney

*   *   *

I am your muse
Pointing the way
I know how lost you have felt
You have the images
And in abundance
You were not planted
In fertile soil
Then uprooted by death and drink
It's understandable that
You lost your way
You're found
I have been waiting here
Rooted
     Upward
       Outward
Look within
A furtive glance
I see your fear
At the threshold of the abyss

It is but the emptiness
Living into the burst
Of words, pictures, ideas, colors
Which tell your story.

–Suzanne Chaumont

*   *   *

I am the resistance that you call the night. I am the two hands you don't recognize. (But they're your hands you know.)

I am the faces of Picasso–the three eyes, the two noses, lips on the side of the face and everything as it should be.

I am confusion and sense. I am the thing you throw away, but without me everything has three eyes and two noses and lips on the side.

And Van Gogh was right with his wavy images of everything blurred and beautiful.

It's raining again, do keep the shades drawn, turn off the lights, and don't get out of bed.

There's coffee in the morning, and music with no paper to read and the eyes on the wall in the faces with their many lips and noses make so much sense.

–Rebecca Geiger

Chapter Five

Listening to Your Writer's Voice

Hëlëne Cixous, Professor at the University of Paris and a most extraordinary writer, warrants your attention. I name her because of her unparalleled gift for language. (She is the Director of the University's Center for Research in Feminine Studies.) Her words leap off the pages of her book. They pulsate and vibrate with a compelling urgency for the reader to keep reading, keep reading.

In her book, *Coming To Writing and Other Essays*, she explores her writing process in great depth. She allows her writing voice to beckon, to wail to her, and to inform her. The result is proof that writing can lead you into enchanted places. This book is a magical incantation.

When Cixous explores the "why" of writing, she says, "Sometimes I think I began writing in order to make room for the wandering question that haunts my soul and hacks and saws at my body; to give it a place and a time; to turn its sharp edge away from my flesh; to give, seek, touch, call, bring into the world a new being who won't restrain me, who won't drive me away, won't perish from very narrowness."

When Professor Cixous speaks to "this new being who won't restrain me," her words slap me in the face. They hit me square in the jaw, for she has pinpointed my vulnerable spot and the vulnerable spot for many women, "voluntary restraint."

Restraint. Why is it that we restrain ourselves? We hide, create excuses and recreate excuses for not writing, for not examining our pages, for not listening to ourselves, for ignoring our writing voice deep inside.

I am not an expert on human behavior, but I know enough about the inner workings of my being to know that when I don't write; when I ignore my writing voice; when I try to quell her, to suffocate her; when I continually refuse to give her permission to surface, to talk, to announce herself, to hear her words, I feel dead.

For many women I know, as well as for myself, restraint equals death; not a literal death, but the type of death in which one's soul perishes, and one's creative voice has no one to speak through. The most acute danger of not listening to this voice is that it deters each of us from ever knowing how to listen to ourselves. When we continue to ignore our voices within, we lose the experience of learning to trust our intuition. The type of trust I am referring to can only be known internally, not rationally.

When we deny our inner writing voice, we also deny ourselves in other ways, for this denial always spills into a woman's life. I urge you to take the time to let your writing voice speak to you; to address you; to inform you, for it has much to tell you.

My writing voice, my work, and my self are fused; and I cannot honestly separate myself, Janet, from Janet, the writer. When I ignore my writing voice; when I ignore those insistent whispers; then, I am choosing to ignore myself. This act always results in devastating emotional consequences.

Writing has always soothed me, and even though it is often frustrating, I constantly return to it for it invariably signifies for me a return to "my source." The quality of my writing does indeed make a difference to me, and I am forever searching for the well-created sentence and paragraph and page; but, it doesn't always appear at will. Even when I write trash, I know that my next sentence can possess diamonds.

The next exercise is a useful vehicle for contacting your writing voice. It is an easy way for you to find out what is slowing you down in your writing (and your life), and finding out how to access your special writing talents.

DIRECTIONS

Make yourself comfortable, close your eyes and take a few breaths. I want you to go deep into yourself and imagine that you are inside your body. Within your body is a special place where you can relax, feel safe and content. I would like you to listen to the whispers inside of you with all of your attention.

Answer the following questions as if the whispers inside of you were speaking directly to you. What do your whispers tell you? So they come from a voice outside of yourself? Another person? A family member? What do you need to pay attention to in your life? What is holding you back? When you are ready, and have listened accurately, write for twenty minutes without stopping. Don't edit your words, just keep writing and always let the pen inform you. Don't concern yourself with the prose, or the form it takes, and try to release any tendency you may have to control the writing.

When you are finished, read it very slowly. Take turns reading it aloud to your partner if you are working with another woman writer. If you are alone, read it to yourself, loudly. The most important aspect of this exercise is to really listen. You'll find an inordinate amount of rich information in this exercise. I urge you to repeat it often.

The samples of writing in this chapter are from many different woman writers and, like the other examples in this book, amaze me.

WOMEN'S VOICES

My writer's voice is also my speaker's voice; it is also my visual/ painter's voice and my intellectual/idea-driven voice. It's the voice of my own experience. It's sometimes loud and clear, sometimes soft and sometimes sad; sometimes my voice will cry. My writer's voice will tell the world all my stories; good and bad; of my childhood and my adulthood; of my pain and sorrows; of the funny times; the sad times; the good times (if I can remember any). It will speak my opinions to the world about the world, both personal and universal. The writer's voice and all the other voices are the passage from the past to the present and the beyond.

Hopefully, they carry me to the edge, and through to the other side and let me share with others my visions, my ideas. It is these multiple voices that continue me on the search for self-discovery, that pushes my boundaries of curiosity.

To be continued in another lifetime–

–Rhoda London

* * *

My writer's voice feels extremely interior, resides in a quiet womb, and is almost silent . . . yet not. It's authentic expression feels profoundly centered, deep, almost not mine. Yet it is, personally me in there. It's a larger Self which is emotionally powerful, elegant, and wise. It reveals the inner truths; something almost divine. Even when talking about dirt and sludge. It reveals the hidden feelings, the murky places in our souls that want to be recognized. It wants to make us whole through inspiration and example. So stories of everyday living come out, but they're universal in themes. The dream, the hope, the uplifting element in life is what most moves me.

–Paula Denman

*   *   *

Right now, I am writing for me and then I share most of it with my writing group. Eventually I'd like to write for a wider audience but I need courage. Who is that wider audience? I haven't defined it yet. I'd like to write poetry, features, maybe a periodic column of observations. And from my group I've discovered I like writing about travels.

First, I have to feel better about my writing–I write many pieces, know what in them I like, and what in them I don't I like. But, I never seem to be able to change what I don't like into something I do so that I would be willing to go public with the piece.

Then, I write for the inner self–a notebook of jottings when my emotions are so close to the surface that they are screaming to be heard. When I write these down, my pen racing as fast as it can, hindered only by the weight of my hand, I often never read them again.

–Jeanne Dorward

*   *   *

I am your writer's voice. I am strong, clear, precise. I am the observer, the listener, the one who sits in the dark on the couch looking out the window at all the tiny lights and cars on the freeway. I lie next to your husband at night and listen to his heart and feel his warm sleeping breath in my hair. I am your writer's voice sandwiched in between your heart and your stomach. I remember things when you remember, I hurt when you do. I sit on the edge of your plate and on the rim of the coffee cup.

I have always been here. It is you who has not allowed me to lean over your shoulder, whisper in your ear. It is you who has kept paper and pencil from me. I am your writer's voice. Rich, full. Sometimes I scream. I get lost in your dreams. I don't know any more or any less than you do. I seek to understand you. Always you. Because I love you.

—Joyce Roschinger

*   *   *

I open my notebook and I'm a child again.
Writing with a pen fatter than my fingers
and letting it drop to recall
the voices that one hears so distinctly as a child.
Not a woman.
The voices will tell you when she was good . . .
she was indeed, very, very, good . . .
as they inspect the roots of your hair
and spray your chest with Chantilly perfume.
And when she was bad. . .
When she was bad. . .
she was just like that girl Nicole,
whose parents spoke German
and wouldn't take her to mass on Sunday.
Fish on Friday.
Mass on Sunday.
Dad working double shifts to put booze in his pocket
and pretzels on the table.
Years ago, I moved to Milwaukee, changed my name,
took a job at a Greek diner
and I opened my notebook.
Writing with a pen I stole from Rexall's,
my fingers fat and mean from the cold
Fat and mean like Milwaukee.
I thought I had buried my beds, incarcerated my dreams,

and wounded my bad luck.
I thought I had opened my notebook for good.
But I was shipped back to the voices and the fat ladies
who begged me to believe in God, Sex, and the Family.
I resent their clever chorus:
Love me. Write me.
Stop betraying me with your cheap cigarettes,
crazy friends and misguided career choices.
But how can I turn away?
Their lives and their perfume are tucked
into my drawers with cachets.
Somewhere I know my life is waiting for me.

–Sandra Stevens

* * *

What I remember is that the truth is revealed in any moment, any circumstance, if one is truly in the present. Fully digesting the experience so all the nutrients can be absorbed, all the nuances are observed and felt. What I remember is that when I come to point (pencil and paper), walk the narrow path, I am confident. I know where I am. I am led forward on the path by my writing; it is my vehicle for travel–for revelation. The lines on the page are the roadways for the pen to travel. If the lines are not there, the very fact of the movement of the pen on the paper provides context. I love this internal focus this direction from within–in contrast to wandering mind. A mind loose in the city of distraction, like a stray dog–lost, disoriented with no master.

Writing teaches me to trust myself; to trust those first feelings.

–Jyoti Haney

* * *

My experiments in creativity are frequently contaminated by the pressure to turn out a worthwhile finished product. These nebulous standards of value, hovering, "out there," somewhere have a paralyzing effect upon my freedom to tell my story by way of mark-making. I face a formidable barrier. I would like to report that I have managed to go beyond the question, "Am I doing this the right way?" Truthfully, questions of this sort plague me constantly. Confronting a blank piece of paper is as terrifying to me as facing the emptiness within myself. It seems I am lacking my own internally generated images, I have lived so much of my life on the surface of appearances that symbols are both terrifying and fascinating. The language of metaphor and symbol is uncharted territory in my work. I am venturing into the chaos of the unknown.

–Suzanne Chaumont

Chapter Six

A Woman's Ritual

I love rituals. I hold fast to my rituals, no matter how absurd they may seem to other people. I embrace my rituals because they offer me solace, comfort, and a time of communion with myself. I believe that a woman's ritual is most potent simply because she chooses to engage in it and she cherishes it just because it is of her own making.

Our rituals may change during our life. We leave them or cling to them at various times in our lives. We are often dedicated to our rituals because the engaging in the ritual, the experience of the ritual, the re-creation of the ritual reminds us of something or some-one in our past. Sometimes, it is the very people who taught us these rituals who serve as catalysts for engaging in the ritual. The ritual is simply the manifestation of our desire to remember that special person. In that case, it doesn't matter so much about the particular ritual, but it does matter that we repeat the steps as we did with *them;* the ritual participants.

I think it is sad that our culture does not engage in rituals that celebrate the times of great meaning in a woman's life; our first period, our first sexual awakening, our discovery of our own cre-ativity, our life's passages. Religions carry within their doctrines the practice of ritual but for many women, these rituals have lost their meaning. Our desire for authentic ritual has lead us on a search for a new way; a way that inspires.

When I was a child, I used to wake up earlier than I would prefer on Sunday mornings because I wanted to engage in my favorite ritual; driving to the bakery with my father. This may seem silly or even mundane but, for me, it was sacred. I looked forward to it all week. I would wash up and quickly get dressed while my father was in the kitchen reading the Sunday paper. He had been up hours waiting for me. We had an intrinsic understanding that this was our ritual. We never verbalized it, or even planned for it, it was just assumed that we would drive together to the bakery. After all, it was Sunday morning.

Although we would always ask my mother if she wanted to come with us, she always declined, knowing that this was our time together. I appreciated her knowing. Off we would go to the bakery to buy bagels, cream cheese, milk, and usually, fresh-baked pastries to accompany the Sunday meal. Sometimes, my dad and I would speak; customarily, our conversations would be about old cars. We would sometimes take a detour to see one (circa 1930, or so) that was buried behind the chain link fence of a car dealer who specialized in vintage automobiles. To this day, I can tell you the year and the name of almost any classic car.

I still cherish those drives. Whenever I visit my parents, my father and I still engage in the same ritual, no matter if we are on the East Coast or the West Coast.

The ritual was important: not for the food; not for the anticipation of the Sunday meal, which we both knew would be pleasant; but because we were together. Our ritual was shared. Even though I try to replicate it on Sunday mornings, it isn't the same, for my dad isn't driving my car, and I don't smell the pungent odor of his cigar.

Rituals offer us more than the pleasure of engaging in a creative and nurturing act. They offer us comfort, and an opportunity to claim time for just ourselves; a lost art.

Sometimes, superstition plays into our rituals. For example, some writers (like myself) write only on legal-sized tablets with a special pen, or eat a particular breakfast, or drink from a designated cup in the morning. All of these acts are potent because we have deemed them *ours*. Rituals are best when each woman selects them for herself–whether it is running a bath, arranging fresh flowers in a child's bedroom, preparing a meal for friends, or running each afternoon at four.

DIRECTIONS

Make a list of each activity you perform each week which you consider a ritual. Don't negate any ideas, even if they seem silly.

Try to recall what the ritual is and write it out as if you were explaining it to someone. When you are finished, think about why you enjoy this ritual so. What is it about this ritual that is so important to you? Where did you learn it? What does it teach you about yourself?

The writing in this chapter does not stick to the suggested directions; and, that is fine. Jeanne Dorward's observations in "Chater Square" recreate a ritual she observed and it is as rich as if she was engaging in the ritual herself. Rebecca Geiger's breakfast ritual with an ex-lover captures a poignant moment between them.

The writers took liberties in the writing of their ritual and I encourage that. I have also taken liberties with my choices of the writing in this book, because I don't subscribe to the one-size-fits-all school of writing. It is not only OK to break the rules, I encourage you to do so. Use my directions as a guide, but always feel free to improvise at will.

The experimentation of style and voice in your work (and in your life, for that matter) is always valid. What matters in the writing, in your work, is that the writing resonates with each writer, striking her chord and reverberating her own truth.

WOMEN'S VOICES

Approximately 6 a.m.

Realize that the paws digging into your chest and the warm tongue licking your eyelids are actually real–not part of that softly woven dream. The cocker spaniel you rescued once upon a time repays you with this. Every day.

Negotiate with Sophie. Promise her the world if only she'll let you sleep ten more minutes. Approximately 6:30 a.m. Another glorious day. Put on your favorite robe . . . OK, it's your only robe, but it's a down robe which you'll need because it's cold out there.

Give Sophie a treat for making you leave your safe flannel sheets so that she can dig holes in your simulated yard and bark at the cats next door. Now walk down the stairs–be sure to trip on that last one. Open the door and there it is. *The New York Times*. Nobody stole it. Remember how annoyed you used to get in the other neighborhood, where you had to get up at 5 a.m. if you wanted to get your paper before someone else did. Brace yourself for the news by making your first pot of coffee–with spring water of course because you don't trust tap water. Reach for a cigarette but remember: *you can quit any time you want.* Flip through the Arts and Leisure section first, then move on to any number of government's atrocities. George Bush addresses a graduating class at a predominantly black college in Virginia, but oddly avoids the issues of racial tension and Civil Rights. Perhaps, Mr. Bush thought that if he didn't mention vetoing the Civil Rights Bill, no one would ask him about it. And surely if students want to make an impression on the president, they will remain seated quietly in their chairs. Act the privileged American and the president might tell you to have a glorious day.

7:15 a.m. Time to go to the bathroom and wash the ink off your face and hands.

–Sandra Stevens

*　*　*

He is so handsome I think. His face is like a neanderthal, or a monkey, and his body is small and compact. He's very trim. At first I thought he was too skinny, but now I see that he's perfect. He has a little mole near his mouth that I like to look at. I think it makes him look smart. The mole and the glasses both make him look smart.

He is my lover. My very handsome, smart, Israeli lover. "You have to take a shower and get dressed," he says, frowning. He takes my hand and leads me into the bathroom where he starts the water. My robe hangs on the back of the door. He bought it for me, not so much out of niceness, but because I was always wearing his. It's a wonderful warm, long, pink, robe.

He watches me as I lean over to check the water. "You have a renaissance figure," he says, laughing, "definitely renaissance."

In Israel he was a soldier. He fought in both the '68 and the '73 wars, and he tells me that his friends died in his arms. Every night before we go to sleep we listen to the short wave radio behind the bed, and again in the morning before we leave. He has a smaller short wave that he sometimes carries in his car. Always, we listen for Israeli radio or BBC.

Sometimes at his house we listen to Israeli folk songs. He tells me that before they went off to fight there was such a feeling of togetherness. The singers would come to perform for the soldiers. He says one woman who is very famous came and sang for them all night long, and the next day they went off to fight.

I don't help him much with breakfast. Mostly I set the table and let him do the work. There is an intensity and a perfection about this breakfast. It's so sensual, like him.

By the time I arrive in the kitchen, he has already pulled out two sesame seed bagels and sliced them in half. "I'll put on the music," I say.

I go to the adjoining room to look through the records. I can't decide between a flute concerto and a modern Israeli folk singer, but I finally go with the folk singer. The music is very nice, very melodic. And the music combined with the man in the kitchen gives everything an exotic air. He has already put lots of feta on one half of both bagels and now he cuts off huge slices of cheddar for the other half. I am not all that hungry, but I know if I don't eat with him or if I cat only half he will be hurt. It won't be the same.

He has made sandwiches out of the bagels and placed them in the microwave. I sing along with the music and even though the songs are in Hebrew, I know all the words. Very soft, sweet music, good for morning.

I take two mugs from the cabinet, one pink, one purple, and pour the coffee, as he removes the bagels from the microwave, putting in their place a cup of milk. When the milk comes to a boil, he pours it over the coffee.

Before we eat, we look at each other, smile, and say, "Bete Avon," and then we eat. I can't tell you how good these bagels are and how wonderful the coffee. They are perfectly hot and the cheese is heaped on and melted so that some of it drips through the hole in the bagel onto the plate. The flavor explodes in my mouth. The feta provides just the right amount of tang and combines with the cheddar and the crunchy bagel in a way that makes each bite a sensation.

We are happy and warm eating our breakfast, and soon he starts telling me stories.

–Rebecca Geiger

* * *

Looking down from my hotel room window, I see Christo's umbrellas once more. Only these are not in the right country at all, they are permanent and they are yellow. And they didn't cost 26 million dollars.

They are there every morning, witnessing the faithful tai chi audience like steadfast sunflowers. Shortly after the breakfast sun has had its orange juice, it smiles down on Chater Square. The participants bend and stretch, like one massive cat, just to loosen the muscles. They go on about their timeless ritual, oblivious to the eager commuters, the new Hong Kong workforce, pulsing through the square. In such a hurry, these new colony workers rush from the Star Ferry and the Metropolitan Rapid Transit, to fill the chambers of commerce, heading for the I.M. Pei bank building and the bastions of capitalism. Mingling among them are those minions of the moneyed classes–they populate the serving class. They wait the tables, sweep the streets, clean the toilets, dust the loos, and generally pick up after the thoughtless and the thoughtful.

But in Chater Square at dawn, the age-old movement holds sway. Each arm stretching to reach the heavens looks like a cat's slowly awakening exercise. There's some ritual here, some rite that reaches back through the ages. One of our group joins them one morning and Marian is welcomed as an ancient practitioner. Though she speaks no Chinese and they no English, their communication transcends the everyday. Her understanding of their ritual is deep within her soul–she could no more explain it than hypothesize why bumblebees can stay airborne.

She mimics their gestures and they welcome her. They understand that her heart is one with them. They ask Marian to step to the front but she demurs, perhaps realizing that there is more to this philosophy than the shadowplay she has permitted herself.

So in Chater Square at dawn the ritual goes on. Long, lean, and lithe, the daily practitioners hone their skills. Each movement highly choreographed, nary a misstep.

–*Jeanne Dorward*

It is a challenge to . . . listen with the heart, to hear the language that lives in the Silence as surely as it lives in the word.

–Marion Woodman, *The Pregnant Virgin:*
A Process of Psychological Transformation
(Toronto, Canada, Inner City Books, 1985, pg. 11).

Chapter Seven

Writing a Woman's Life: Trust vs. Fear

Many people live in fear. Our fears hold us back from making important changes in our lives and from taking the initiative to follow our hearts instead of our minds. Opportunities to transform our fears, to transform our insecurities, to make peace with ourselves, and to move ahead in our writing and in our lives constantly make themselves available to us. The loss of our job or relationship, financial upheaval, and internal turmoil all signal us to pay attention. They provide excellent catalysts and they help us to move forward into a new life, to re-examine our priorities, to re-invent ourselves anew. Yet, we often fight these changes and choose to remain stuck, unable to move, unable to call upon our energies to rebuild our lives. We blanket ourselves with our fears and, as a consequence, are often crushed by their weight.

It has taken me a long time to allow myself to descend into my fear; to trust that the fear could hold great teachings for me, if I was willing to listen. I try not to panic. When it is over, I realize that I was provided with an opportunity to view my interior world. My writing has given me the courage to face my fears. But this has not been an easy process nor a quick one, and I have the scars to prove it.

It is the willingness to listen that has made all the difference in my life. I can't honestly say that I welcome entry into the shadow side, for it is always uncomfortable; but, when I experience this dark side, I remind myself that I *know* how to navigate and I *will* surface when it's time.

My writing usually reveals to me "How I really feel" about a job, a relationship, a friendship, or a life choice. That realization is quite different from "How I think I should feel," and I am careful to make that distinction.

I believe that I can offer to you useful insights about the darker phases in a woman's life. All women experience this bleakness at some time in their life. Remember, that you are not alone. Some women "put on a happy face" but this is mental suicide, for they take the risk of losing themselves by denying their internal reality. The darkness is harsh but it always gives way to the light.

Writing down one's feelings in a diary, tracking each day as if you were an observer, recording your dreams, can all be very, very helpful. Each woman has her own method that works best for her and it is up to her to discover it.

All I know is that when I remain silent, I invariably pay a physical and emotional price. My body revolts and I feel ill. Remaining in silence about the areas in your life that ignite you is a horrible form of psychological self-torture.

We live in a culture where remaining silent, being a "nice girl," pleasing others without regard to how we truly feel, is rewarded. From an early age, women are taught to please and we have become oblivious to our own true wants and needs. We don't trust our voices because we never pay attention to them. We don't admit to anyone including ourselves, what we truly want because of fear of reprisal. Sometimes, we don't voice the truth because we don't have a person in our life who is available to listen, whom we can trust.

Writing can be an "exorcism" since the writing process helps to document the anger, fear, and disappointment that a woman feels. Allowing yourself to record those feelings serves as a powerful alternative to self-destruction through silence, drinking, or other abuses. We have the choice to listen to our inner silence and see what we can learn from it. What does it want to tell us? What can our silences reveal to us?

One woman in my workshop told me that she was frequently scared to address her silent voices, for she thought it would overwhelm her since she has been silent for so long. She didn't want to hear what her pen had to tell her. Creating a safe place to listen to that silence is an all-important step to understanding our internal lives. What you choose to do with that information is always up to you.

I suggest that, if you are writing about some aspect of your life that is painful, pay attention, stick with the process, and make time for yourself in safe and peaceful surroundings. In order to listen to yourself, you have to create that time and place. Don't distract yourself by busying yourself. Write, take walks, try to get away for a day or two, get a massage, or just sit in the tub. Plan your own healing.

Frequently, women in my writing workshops cry when reading their work aloud, particularly when they write about the silences in their lives. Their hands shake, their voices are hesitant and they are visibly nervous. If you are reading your work to another person and feel emotional, don't apologize and don't let the emotions stay inside. It is all right to express yourself. The actual reading of the material is often very soothing, and when it is finished, you may experience a sense of calm. Take breaths, read slowly; don't let yourself rush through the words.

DIRECTIONS

I would like you to take out a sheet of paper and complete this sentence: "I am _____ 's (*your name here*), most hateful and negative writing voice and I want to tell her _____ ." Complete the sentence and add as much prose as you like. Write for at least ten minutes and don't stop to edit or to censor your writing. This writing exercise is a powerful exorcism. I urge you to expunge all the negativity that fills your head.

Don't read what you've written, but take it and crumble it up. Put it in a fireproof pot and burn it. Burn the pages of negativity, squash its life and let it burn. Burn your negativity out of your mind and out of your being. Make sure you burn the paper in a fireproof receptacle and in a well-ventilated area of your house or apartment. An alternative method which is just as potent is to burn the writing and throw the ashes in the sea, or over a mountaintop. Sometimes, I save my burned writing in a pot and take it to a beach a few days later to toss into the sea. It is a powerful release, and a cleansing; and an opportunity to make magic.

Some of my students have told me that one of the most harmful blocks in their writing is that the negative voices in their heads sabotage their work. These critical voices actively detour a woman from feeling good about herself and prevent her from engaging in the creative process. These negative voices always halt a woman's writing and, no wonder. They attack her self-esteem and confidence, empower her fears, and preside over her in most insidious ways.

I am not suggesting that you discount those fears. On the contrary, I think these fears need to be given a voice. It is only when you allow these negative voices to express themselves that you can manage them instead of having them manage you. Don't try to avoid your fears, for they will only keep you shackled. Let your words lead you out.

Whenever you feel blocked in your writing (or in your life) take a few moments at your computer or your typewriter or pull out a pen and paper and write a message to yourself from your inner negative voices. Let those voices shriek and wail. *Do not read the message!* Crumble it into a ball, set fire to it, or throw it away. This exercise is very, very healing.

DIRECTIONS

I want you to close your eyes and clear your mind. I want you to think about your silence. See it, hear it, feel it, and just listen to it. When you are ready, write down what your impressions are about your silence. What does it look like? Does it have a name? What does it want to tell you? What are the words that you have not spoken? What do you need to say? When will you be ready to speak your truth? What stops you?

Write for twenty minutes and give your inner silence an opportunity to join you, to be present in your life.

WOMEN'S VOICES

Reunion
Descent
  into
    the
      realm
beneath the blankness
Tendrils
  of
    the
      truth
Sending light energy
into the void of fatigue.

–Suzanne Chaumont

*   *   *

"It's time to die!" my inner voice whispered. . . . "Repent!" the man on the TV had said. "Repent . . . change direction . . . Renounce. . . . old habits and ideas!" "It's time . . . ," I whispered. "Let's see what loving this man *really* means . . . ."

I sigh and resign myself to another death; death of the will, the stubborn need to control, diligence at all costs . . . I shiver inside. It's scary. There's no one with me now. It's an empty, cold and hollow place, dark, spacious, quiet . . . . My old companions have gone. I look around and squint. I see an old woman in black holding a candle. She mourns the death of her loved ones; she mourns the death of an old friend, old ways. She gives me a gentle grin with her eyes and the sweet corners of her mouth, the way only old ladies can do. She steps silently to my side.

I look into the candle. It flickers and leaps and waves at me! There are dancers wriggling their bodies up and down, laughing and smiling! "I thought the fire was supposed to be dangerous." They giggle, "Oh, it's just another lie they told you. Come on! Jump in!" I jump into the fire and melt instantly. I am one with the other flames. We laugh and wiggle and leap up and down. We sway and pray and whistle. The heat feels so soothing and rich. The flames give me life. I am full of energy and excitement in a way I've never known. And to think I'd been afraid to touch something so beautiful and free. All at once, I explode into a spark and a *pop!* then I shot out in all directions.

–Mary Ellen Rescigno

*   *   *

She had her hair frosted the day before, a new style, bobbed short in the back, longer on the sides. It was summer in Santa Barbara. She was tanned and trim from her daily tennis outings and anyone observing her would see a confident young woman in her late twenties.

She chose the black and white print cotton pique sun dress from her closet. Yes, this would do, along with her black patent leather sandals. Dinner was at eight that evening at the home of her husband's senior law partner. The children were at the babysitter's and she had two hours now to prepare her mind for what she imagined could be a challenging dinner conversation. She picked up the current issue of *Time* magazine from the topaz colored glass coffee table. Her husband's subscription arrived every week, but she had barely lifted a page. Now, should she go for the politics section or current events? As she began to flip through the pages, her heart beat faster, her eyes blurred. "What if I am asked to give my opinion!–What if they ask me to say more?" What if she embarrassed her husband? What if she opened her mouth and had no voice at all?

–Jyoti Haney

*   *   *

My writer's voice wants to tell me to keep writing, to keep exploring, to push the limits. I must not stop. I must pursue, I must give myself permission to write.

My writer's voice has been silenced for so long. It is like Rip Van Winkle awakening from a long sleep. I have to stretch it slowly, gradually build up its strength and flexibility. My voice is scratchy at first, after years of silence and disuse. I have to clear it several times, stop and start over. Sometimes the words come out haltingly as I struggle to remember the vocabulary. Sometimes, not often, they rush out in a torrent, as if the spigot were suddenly released and the water in the pipe gushes out until the pipes are drained.

Sometimes the words ring clear and true. They are truth, they've captured what I want to say. Sometimes they're barely audible, the right words don't come and people can't understand me.

But as I practice, my voice gets stronger. The vocal chords start to become more flexible–they resonate with the stored-up sounds, that want to emerge to be set free. I need to take care of this voice, to nurture it, to exercise it. Now that it's reawakened, I dare not let it hibernate or go into a coma again.

–Jeanne Dorward

* * *

I've been silent so long, I've forgotten the language. I've forgotten I know the truth–the true language of Being–my deepest thoughts about life. There's a deep place, dark, unexplored that can only be brought to the light through writing. Writing is the way out of the depths. So many words are given away in idle conversation before I have known them truly myself through the intimate act of writing. What is that fear of being truly intimate with one's self? The power, the richness of that?

Don't shush me! I will not speak in a whisper! You treat me as if I should be ashamed to speak–as if my words could cause you to be banished, sent off in exile where I then would only be let out behind thick stone walls, the words locked up then to ensure that they would not be stolen and whisked away to the outside world. Do you think you would be hung or burned at the stake if I was discovered, if I was allowed to rise to my full stature? I will no longer be silenced so you might as well unlock the door to the inner chambers and throw away the key. Allow me to come out in the open to be revealed; I have volumes of unspoken wisdom to share with you, with the world!

–Jyoti Haney

Chapter Eight

Mothers and Daughters: Understanding the Template of Our Lives

I have my mother's body; long tapered hands, mismatched ribs, sharp hip bones and legs which will never suit me. I have my mother's mind, full of inquiry, probing, questioning, curious. I have both loved and hated my mother; sometimes simultaneously.

After six months in her womb, I wanted to be released into the world; and, although the medical establishment preferred otherwise, I was born three months premature, defying the drugs which raced through my mother's body to prevent my early arrival. It was the 1950s and I was very lucky to survive during a time when most premature babies died.

Carl Jung said that, "Every mother contains her daughter in herself and every daughter her mother, and that every woman extends backwards into her mother and forwards into her daughter." I really love this quote for I feel it is true not only for me, but for all women. The mother/daughter web is wound tightly with each woman-daughter-mother; and separating from *her*, the mother, to be our own person is one of the most engaging, difficult, powerful, confusing, and liberating processes that a woman will encounter along her way.

Naomi Ruth Lowinsky, author of *The Motherline, Every Woman's Journey to Find Her Female Roots*, writes eloquently about the mysteries of mother and daughter–the Motherline. She uses the term "looping" to explain "the associative process by which we pass through our own experiences to understand that of another. . . . If our female experience is to be meaningful for us, we must awaken to the female depths from whence we came." Her book is a tribute to every mother and daughter. The need for mothers and daughters to connect and to share that "longed for gift between women: a daughter's affirmation of her mother, a mother's affirmation of her daughter," speaks to us all.

Many women I know from the baby boom generation grew up in the 1950s and were raised by young mothers of the Dr. Spock era. My mother was a typical woman of that time. She had two toddlers at home, a traveling husband, a sharp mind, and loneliness to fill her days when she was only in her twenties. She grew up in a large family with four sisters and two brothers. Since she was favored by her father, she had to pay a price for that attention. Her mother, who rejected her "marriage-matched" husband, likewise, found fault with my mother no matter how "good" she was.

Oddly, it was my grandmother who began to write to me when I was in graduate school, sending me notes of encouragement, cards, and pieces of her memoirs. It was as if she could only send her love through me to reach my mother. I was the conduit for the affection that she could never give to my mother. How tragic for both of them.

Our longing to be known by our mothers is an integral part of every woman's journey. We long to "be known" by and "to know" our mothers so that we can experience our relationship on a much deeper level.

I use writing as a healing tool with my students, and ultimately for healing myself. When I first introduced the writing exercise about one's mother, I wasn't sure what the reaction would be. I knew of the abusive relationships which existed for some and of the chasms which separated so many women from their mothers. But, this exercise was very powerful and potent and the women in my group frequently talked about how insightful it proved to be for them.

DIRECTIONS

Close your eyes. I want you to imagine that you are able to step into the body of your mother during the time that she was pregnant with you. Try to recreate what she was feeling, and thinking. Where is she? What year is it? What are her concerns? In what month in her pregnancy is she? Try to imagine what her frame of mind was.

Try to recall the time of year and the house or apartment in which she lived. What does she want to tell you, her unborn child?

When you are ready, leave her and reclaim yourself. Take a moment to clear your connection with her. Take fifteen minutes and write down everything you can see, sense, touch, or intuit about your visualization, no matter how trivial it may seem. Commit to paper what you have seen and felt in any way that seems authentic to you. It is sometimes useful to get started by writing a letter to her, or writing from her vantage point in dialogue. As in all of the exercises in this book, it doesn't matter what form you choose, only that you write your truth.

I think that this is a wonderful exercise to do with other women. You may want to invite your women friends to come together to write to you. Some women in my workshops have mailed the material they wrote to their mothers. Use the work for whatever purpose that you deem appropriate.

If you decide to work with other women, ask them to bring a picture of their mothers to help with the writing. If you work alone, I would encourage you to use photographs of your mother and childhood photographs to boost your writing.

Photographs are a marvelous source for writing autobiography. If you want to take out photographs of important people in your life during some of these exercises, then do so. The photographs often prompt forgotten memories.

WOMEN'S VOICES

I see my mother standing, facing the kitchen sink, doing the dishes. Dark clothing, dark hair, shoulder length. My two towheaded older sisters, standing near and between her legs–fighting, dodging, poking each other. She is pregnant with me, and engrossed in chores. Thinking, planning, wondering how they'll afford another baby and how she'll make her energy stretch. Methodical hand motions round and round the inside of tumblers. Sudsy hot water and soothing steam.

My mother sits in the black rocking chair with me in her arms. A dark-haired baby girl. Another girl. Will my father ever get the son he craves? She cuddles me and talks to me in the sweet voice, now reserved for grandchildren and visiting infants. The voice my grandmother gave her; the voice my sister Deborah inherited. The high, high voice. She feeds me and cuddles me and rocks me waiting for me to slip to sleep so she can get on with the supper chores before my dad gets home.

Elizabeth, my grandmother's maid, has come to clean and watch the other two girls. Elizabeth came again when my sister Lauren was born. I remember her manner, brusque and businesslike. Her very German accent and her rimless glasses which scared me. She wore an apron with big pockets and she seemed huge. I thought I would fall into her pocket and never get out and be lost in her cold manner.

It was spring when I was born and the trees were in bud–but not blooming. The daffodils were up and out. The long New England winter was gone and Easter was near. We would get new dresses and go to church with hats and white gloves. We had to behave, but Matty, my sister, would pinch me in church or make me laugh and I'd get a poison look from Gram. My mother would poke Matty hard on the leg with a steel finger. She knew who was the troublemaker. She didn't even look at Matt–she'd stare straight at Dr. Anderson as he gave his sermon, an attentive face.

I thought my mother was so beautiful when she was dressed for church. She'd wear a hat and her good jewelry and those miraculous high heels. The ones we could never use for dress up.

–Nancy Wilson

*   *   *

Look at your face in the mirror and wonder
if you will resemble your mother as you grow older.
Look at your face quietly. You have her soft brown
eyes that turn green in daylight.
You are not a smiler. Like your mother and her mother.
In all of your pictures, you do not smile. Your baby
pictures show a mouth that is set, that says,
"I am here." Nothing more. Nothing less. Look closer.
Your face is slightly round. No high cheekbones here.
Your nose is definitely our mother's especially when you
are angry.
Pull your hair away from your face.

What did your mother see the first time she saw you?
Did she see your father as she traced your mouth with her
finger?
Did she see a hint of herself as she smoothed your
eyebrows, counted your fingers and toes to make sure that
you were all there?
And when she gently brushed the hair away from
your tiny face, did she wonder, "What will this child be
like when she grows up?"
Listen closely.
"Your face is a map of your life." you hear your mother
say softly.

That is why she holds your face in her hands before she
kisses you.
Close your eyes.
Imagine what your mother looks like. The color of her
hair, the cool roundness of her face.
The grooves and lines around her mouth. What her skin feels
like when you kiss her on her cheek.
Now open your eyes.
What did you see?

—Joyce Roschinger

*　　*　　*

June 17, 1991—Part One

   Glad I'm me. Glad is a sweet little word, a sort of innocent word.
(I'll try to forget about Glad Bags.) It seems "glad" was a word
Mom used when we kids were growing up on Dewes Street. She
might have said to Florence Rossiter across the back yard fence,
"I'm so glad it's sunny. Now my tulips will thrive. I've planted
yellow ones all along here." And then she would have pointed from
the top to the bottom of our long yard.
   Mom was quite the pointer. It seems her index finger was always
extended out from the others, pointing at something or someone or
shaking in the direction of one of us in jest or flabbergast. We kids
had more fun teasing Mom about her pointing! It's rare that we get

to see that finger now that it's bent with arthritis. She keeps her hands hidden in pockets most of the time. It may look nonchalant to strangers. There are plenty of reminders in family photographs, though, that provide precious moments of laughter.

I *am* glad I'm me and that I was born to my mother. My field of mental vision clicks onto various memories of her as if powered by slow motion remote control. Mom and me having macaroni and cheese for lunch, just the two of us. (Where were my sisters?) Mom washing chocolatey bowls, beaters, and spoons after I licked them practically clean. Mom vacuuming and me dusting. (We don't call her "Wisk" for nothing.) Mom and me sitting together on the porch swing–she hemming the gathered skirt of teensy purple flowers she made for me to wear to Meredith's birthday party, she secretly pretending that my favorite Mr. Salty pretzel sticks are cigarettes.

The mental remote stops in our back yard on Dewes Street. It's a lovely, hot suburban Chicago summer day. The lawn is freshly mowed, flawlessly green. Mom has just finagled me intro trying on the white "wedding dress" she has made for me. She has cut a number of beautiful white roses from her garden, arranging them nicely and placed them into my hands. I can hardly believe from this vantage point that she is placing a headdress and veil on my nine-year-old head, pinching my pale cheeks and calls for my father who is standing by with his camera. Click. Click. Click. And the caption in the family album that preserves the memory is captioned, "Beautiful bride." Funny that I chose to wear white for none of my three failed marriages in real life.

June 18, 1991–Part Two

"Everything was fine, like clockwork. It was a lot easier than with Chris. I had a kidney infection when she was born, and I was really sick. But with you, everything went just fine. It had nothing to do with you, honey. You were perfect! And when the doctor said, 'It's a girl!' I was so happy."

"Didn't it hurt, Mom?"

"No, it didn't hurt very much. Of course it hurt, but you don't remember the pain afterwards."

"I was born vaginally. Did they give you drugs?"

"Of course! Whatever they gave in those days. Maybe that's why it didn't hurt very much."

"Do you remember my birth, actually?"

"I think I do. I was kind of in and out of it."

"And then what happened? What happened after I was born? Was it right after I was born? Did you get to hold me? Look at me?"

"It happened right after you were born. Right after the doctor said, 'It's a girl.' All of a sudden, I couldn't feel anything on my right side. Then they took you away."

Oh, gees. I can just see the nurses whisking me away before my mother gets a chance to look at me, hold me, before I am cradled in her ready hands. And off I went!–into the nursery with the other wailing babies. All alone in the little crib. If at three moments old my consciousness was somehow aware, my tears were heartfelt, not only signaling wet diapers or parched throat. I imagine I truly missed being inside my mother where we both knew safety.

–Cary Davis

* * *

Tribute to Frances Durning Wagenhals

Born September 21, 1902

Died October 12, 1991

This is a time to speak about my mother; what she has given to me, what she has meant to me and the parts of her that live in me as well as others of her progeny. There is so much that this initial task of consolidation seems overwhelming. It is easy to begin with the obvious, that she gave me life. My gratitude for that alone is unspeakable; there is not a life of anyone whom I have known that I would trade for mine. My own has been so special, so uniquely perfect, and that this might not have been so, indeed rests upon the truth that she and my father united together to form me; she was only 19, (18 when she married), a child with a child.

My mother's physical strength and her boundless energy were always a source of wonder to me. Everything she did she did quickly, and everything she did she did well. I look upon my own life and I find that, indeed, these traits have somehow penetrated into my being effortlessly and visibly. She was up late and arose early; I cannot recall her ever lounging or resting when I was a child. She kept an immaculate and ordered house for all of us, and she did this without help, either hired or from her children. She very kindly allowed us to live our childhoods without the burden of household chores, which for whatever reason, she held a strong conviction, were her responsibility. I sometimes felt guilty, particularly over the hand ironing, and surprisingly, of my adult household tasks that is my favorite.

She was a devoted and loyal woman. She adored my father and has had to bear the pain of life without him for almost forty years. Having four children, with a decade between her two daughters and two sons, demanded from her an intensity of preoccupation for childcare that extended into my adolescence. Her social life was very limited until her children's needs became less demanding.

I truly believe that my mother did not consider nor appreciate her own goodness. Perhaps that is hard for anyone to do. She was so generous and so giving in so many ways to all of us; her gifts were always unconditional. I do not think that my own giving could have had that quality within it, had I not received this from my mother over and over again. The financial security that Bob and I currently enjoy has its beginnings in her generosity; what a privilege it is to live without financial strain.

But, of all of her contributions to my life, the one I value most warmly and tenderly is the wonderful part she played in the lives of each of our children. They all adore her and for good reason. That each one of them has lots of "alone time" with her has been enormously satisfying to me, provided them with immeasurable richness and contributed immensely to my own ability to be a grandmother.

My mother has outlived her husband, her eldest son, his eldest son, her two brothers, and her four sisters, the majority of her friends, and, sadly, her own will to live. It is my wish that she will live long enough for me to present this tribute to her personally.

I read this to my mom on December 11, 1988. My brother was with us. She was then 86. She cried often, saying, "I don't know why I am crying." We all laughed and cried together; it was a sweet and tender highlight of my life.

–Neenie Bradford

* * *

My father's mother was named Bertha Helen, and she died when he was only five. She disappeared very quickly, and no one explained to my dad where she was or what was going on. Maybe this is why later he liked so much to explain things.

One day they told him she'd died, and although they took him to the funeral he wasn't allowed to view the body, or really properly say goodbye. None of us know a lot about her, but we have photographs, and patchy stories from my father's brother. She remains an enigma. She was not beautiful, but in the photos, looks very feminine, and very romantic. She wears soft dresses, long and flowing, light and breezy. She was apparently very smart and was trying to start a canning business, when she became ill.

There is something so mysterious about her. The photographs and the few stories leave so much unsaid. I think of her often, and wonder and hope that her spirit's in me, and that maybe she is watching over all of us.

–Rebecca Geiger

* * *

Mom and I sat in one of the several overstuffed sofas that encircled hooded fireplaces. Biting her inside lower lip, Mom watched the door to the lodge and methodically pushed back the cuticles on her nails.

"Listen baby," she whispered as Susan and Rita entered the room, "Don't tell my friends that you're my daughter, okay?"

My mother was one of the pioneers of the feminist movement, and I one of its casualties. She, like millions of other women in the 60s and 70s rebelled against a stifling social role. She felt cheated in life, enslaved to her husband and children by her coerced role as caretaker. The patriarchy became her enemy and men became her target. Motherhood was no longer a blessing–it symbolized bondage–and I represented her pain.

Motherhood in the 50s took place during a time when "feminist" was not part of our daily dialogue; divorce was an unthinkable act; and blacks were referred to as Negroes. The women of America were busy raising Spock babies and tap dancing around men's egos.

The windless air of the 50s began to stir, and with it the dawning of a new philosophy for child rearing. Many mothers were teaching their sons and daughters to claim their dreams as tools for success. I learned from my mother that it's our imagination that empowers our dreams. She told me, "If our mind can see it we can be it."

I remember one day Mom instructed me to close my eyes and to imagine with all my might what I wanted to be. I closed my eyes so tightly my face contorted. The more tightly I shut my eyes the better the vision, I thought. I arched my back, and squared my tiny shoulders, "I'm a storymaker," I stated.

"A storymaker!" She laughed scooping me into her arms. "Well, my darling, then a maker of stories you shall be."

In the early years of my childhood my mother's laughter came easily. She said laughing caused our brains to release magic endorphins that swam through the lifeblood of our veins, and uplifted our spirits. I wasn't exactly sure how that worked until one day I saw her tears turn into laughter after suggesting she let her magic dolphins go swimming. I knew that her potion worked, and that she had given me the secret elixir. It's laughter that heals our souls and relieves our pain.

The panoramic view of the Sierras, the overstuffed sofas, nor the warmth of the fire could ameliorate my anguish that night my mother asked me not to reveal our relationship. Her request hit hard. My mind whirled with questions and my heart struggled for answers. I remember her muffled voice telling me that she preferred I call her Sheela. "After all, that is my name," she said. "Titles, like Mom and wife only keep women in bondage . . . . You're seventeen for heaven's sake . . . you must cut the apron strings." Eventually the pounding in my chest subsided and my vision cleared enough to focus on her friends. I managed to nod during the introduction, but my thoughts were on those piercing words which severed the core of my existence. "Why?" I asked, "Why can't you be my mother?"

My mother's involvement with the movement soon dominated every aspect of her life. Her newfound network of support allowed her to declare feelings that lay dormant for half-a-lifetime. She awakened to a passion that intoxicated her soul with bliss, pain, anger, and enormous rage. She directed her rage exclusively towards men. "They were the workers of iniquity," she said, "the puppeteers and masters of manipulation." I'll never forget her horror-stricken look of betrayal when I told her of my plans to marry. "How can you be so loyal to the patriarchy?" she wailed.

It took years for my mother to acknowledge my marriage. She could not accept that I, through my own volition, had become part of the very institution she'd been opposing for more than a decade. To her, men were the enemy. "Men are made up of every evil entity that ever existed," she proclaimed one day to my husband. Through the years, hateful words spewed from their mouths creating between them a verbal war zone that left our relationship smoldering in the crossfire.

The birth of my son in 1982 rekindled a forgotten intimacy lost somewhere in the wake of a new revolution. Mom and I now shared an affinity housed in the realm of motherhood. Our renewed alliance evolved into more of a sisterhood, than that of a mother and a child. It was during this time I learned of the woman inside my mother. And, it was during this time when I began to truly know and understand the magnitude of her pain.

There are times, at the end of a very long day, after I've tucked my son in, I sit with my feet propped on the hearth and warm my hands on a cup of hot chamomile tea. I look into the glowing flames of the fire and see images of my mother. She's holding a child. Her eyes are glistening with happiness and she and the child are laughing. The golden flames flicker with green and blue hues and a different image appears. The child is gone and I can no longer hear their laughter. Anger has carved lines around her mouth and her pain embodies this countenance. Sorrow seeps from her eyes, like hot lava flowing down a mountainside, slowly making its way over her cheekbones. Bit by bit it melts her image, stripping it of life and reducing her beauty to hollow impressions of the past. I close my eyes . . . tightly, and I whisper, "Release your magic dolphins."

—Valerie Walker

* * *

One

The memories I have of my mother reveal a harshness in her personality. I long to have recollections which paint a picture of caring ways and gentle moments, but try as I might, that is not what I remember. . . . I am four years old playing in the backyard with Johnny, my little brother. My mother goes into the house telling me to look after him. I am feeling very proud to be left in charge . . . suddenly Johnny is tumbling over . . . I can't get to him in time . . . there's blood all over his wrist. I'm running to get my mother. She screams, "I told you to watch him!" Now she's locked me out of the house. . . . I am so humiliated that the neighbors can see my shame.

There is a part of me even now, who wants to explain that I did watch my brother very carefully. There is a child who still wonders if perhaps it was her fault after all. There are many such memories of my mother and I can only speculate as to what inner pressures she experienced during my early childhood. I sense deep within my own psyche that the demands of mothering three small children extracted a heavy toll on her personhood. Something was very wrong.

Two

. . . My mother and I are alone in the living room . . . she is playing the piano, now the violin, and now the cello. She has magical abilities to make this music! Why does her playing take on a frantic edge? What could be wrong? The scene takes on a haunting quality . . . little girl on the floor watching her mother switch from one instrument to another. What were my mother's dreams? Would that I had access to the diary she never kept. Another memory emerges: every detail still vivid; my mother screaming at me not to call her Mommy, "My name is Marilyn. I have a name, Marilyn, Marilyn, Marilyn!" I remember being so stunned and puzzled. . . .

Three

Another fleeting image. . . . I am five years old, alone in my bedroom struggling to dress myself in a red cotton dress with a white organdy pinafore. I recall so clearly my pride at accomplishing this tedious and lengthy task, only to discover that I have the pinafore on backwards, with the bow in front. I hear the sound of my mother's crying just down the hallway, the hollowness of my father's voice. My childlike sensibilities are so sharply attuned to the despair which leaks out of my parents' bedroom. Their efforts to contain the secret of my mother's illness parallels my redoubled efforts to get ready for school all by myself, like a "big girl."

Next scene . . . I am seven years old, dry-eyed, opening the front door to greet the visitors attending my mother's funeral. I am the oldest, the only one allowed to attend the service. . . the coffin is closed . . . she can't be in that box (breast cancer ravaged her body and she weighed less than 70 pounds at the time of her death). . . . My earliest recollection of the "Our Father" set to music . . . the fragments of another song, "Guardian Angels Around My Bed" . . . I am strangely comforted by the image of angels, though I am stoic in my efforts to remain unaware of my mother in that box. How can that be?

–Suzanne Chaumont

*   *   *

The pregnancy test was positive. It was July 1972. I would be sixteen in September. *Roe v. Wade* would come down from the Supreme Court the following January, but even if abortion had been available to me that summer I don't think I would have chosen it. I was angry, alone and adrift. I wanted a child of my own to love. Having a child was my way of asserting my independence, a way of claiming my adulthood (or so I thought). The pregnancy was a means of open defiance against my parents. Abortion would have meant surrender and defeat.

With the pregnancy I felt I had some ammunition–some leverage against my mother. I called to tell her the news in the hopes she would now have no recourse but to sign the papers allowing me to marry my boyfriend. She still refused. At this point communication ceased. But as time passed I didn't care whether I married or not. My mother's wishes and demands were no longer of concern to me. I was going to have a baby. I was going to live my life. Nothing else mattered.

My son was born in late January of 1973. The labor was short and relatively easy. I did not enjoy my pregnancy or the delivery as so many women say they do today. "New Age" labor and delivery techniques were unknown in Texas at that time. I was treated in a brutal, objectified manner–I felt like meat on the table. To this day I refuse to be treated for any physical ailment by a male physician. In retrospect, I know what I was experiencing was discrimination–discrimination based on my youth and the fact that the father of my child was Hispanic.

To my surprise, my son's arrival brought about an emotional upheaval for me. He was so tiny and red and beautiful. And he was demanding as all newborns are. He needed love and constant attention. Quickly I realized I was not adequately prepared to meet his needs either emotionally or financially. This is when I discovered I was still a child myself. I loved him so much and yet I knew I was not ready to be a mother. Not without help.

I called my mother in the hopes she would allow me to come home with my baby. I had forgotten how cruel and mean-spirited she could be. When I explained my situation to her she told me she'd have to "think it over." She kept me waiting three days. Mother was the type who would go to any lengths to exert her control over you and get her way. In the end she prevailed and I was utterly crushed by her. Her edict was that I could come home on the condition of leaving my child elsewhere–she did not care where. She simply wouldn't have him in her house.

I faced the most difficult decision of my life. How does one reconcile oneself to such a decision? How do we continue to live when our very spirits have been broken? Leaving my son was a decision based on survival–simple, basic, primal survival–both his and mine. In that moment, I knew if I stayed in that place I would die–either by my own hand or that of another. And so I chose to leave him with his father's people while I returned to mine.

His loss has been the greatest wound I have had to endure. It is a spiritual wound as well as emotional. It goes to my very soul. I had gone from believing I was a woman to realizing I was still a child back to *knowing in my very bones* I was a woman. It was a transformative experience–a journey I could not deny. And yet deny it I did for this is what was required of me by my family. Thus began the life I was to live for 18 years–a life based on lies, secrecy, and deceit.

Suffering so as I did at such an early age gave me strength and resilience. Great suffering leads to great strength, if one has the courage to face it. I learned the value of finding and relying on an inner authority. I have had to create my own vision and find my own voice. For years I tried to forget and could not. My love for him was too great. At last I came to a place where I knew I could not continue without finding him and reclaiming my true life. Thus it came to pass that I was able to meet my son. We have been together now three years.

It could be said that mine was an unnecessary tragedy, for a tragedy is what it was. The irony is that all I wanted was a life of my own, unfettered by the demands and expectations of a strong-willed mother. And what I got was a life bound by lies, determined by the desires of another. I feared death and insanity. I experienced a living death strangled by a deep depression. I feared living my life without the loving support of my family. I discovered only too late that I lost that family not after their deaths, but on that fateful day when I returned to that house without my son.

Only by reclaiming my past and reclaiming my son have I been able to find peace and the strength to forgive. For me, the task has been not to forget, but to *remember*. The wound itself, which even now will ever be with me, is the source of all my power and my strength.

(Portions of this piece were originally written in 1988, prior to the reunion. Today, Shelly is much happier in her heart and her spirit.)

–Shelly Compton

Chapter Nine

Special People in a Woman's Life

My life has been significantly altered by the people who have entered, departed, visited, and remained to participate in some manner in my life. These people have offered me inspiration, joy, insight, and laughter and sometimes have dragged me down to the depths of the dark.

I have relied on a small yet consistent array of people, both men and women, throughout my life. Although I have moved across the country three times, I have a group of people who always accompany me psychologically, wherever I am living.

A few of my ex-lovers are still my close friends. They were and are my male counterparts and the comfort we share of being known, loved, and understood has survived the years although our passion did not. Gary, Richard, Michael, and Paul have taught me a great deal about loving and understanding the opposite sex. They have helped me tremendously and I am fortunate to have their friendships.

There are very few people who really know me and I think that is true for many of us. It is an extraordinary gift of friendship to share yourself with another person without holding back out of fear. Friends don't make judgments and they love you no matter what.

My women friends are split up geographically between the West and the East coast. However, all of these women share common bonds, besides their friendship with me. They are strong women, willful, spirited, competent, and tender.

People arrive in my life in odd ways. I met Carol in the library of the offices of Condé Nast Publications while she and I were both conducting research. We met, loved each other instantly and have remained friends for years. It was Carol who changed my life in a profound way, for she was the person who encouraged me to become a college teacher. She was a professor, and she propelled me into the academic domain.

Marlene and I are sisters, and she has given me her grand gift of friendship, love, implicit understanding, support, and always truth-telling. She is a true sage woman.

Sandi is a public relations executive in New York. She and I have known each other for years. We met during a job interview and subsequently found out that we had attended the same college and dated the same man. Even though she lives 3,000 miles away, we have maintained a deep connection.

Mallory, a prominent doctor in Philadelphia, has known me since I was thirteen years old. We have shared vacations, boyfriends, and an appreciation for each other's talents. Whenever autumn arrives, I am always reminded of the drives that we would take together to the countryside in Rhode Island to pick apples, drink wine, and speak candidly about our lives. Liz, my college roommate and I have grown up together as well. I know I have her support, advice, and love forever.

I honor my friends and I am grateful that they are in my life. Donna, Mimi, Lauren, Jyoti, Liz, Marlene, Mallory, Sandi, Carol, Debbie, Yvonne, all form a coterie of friends who are my shields, and my companions. I know I can call upon them whenever I need advice, encouragement, an understanding ear, and a familiar voice.

Although I know many people, I am still obsessively private. When my spirits soar, I am inclined to spend more time in the outside world. Usually, when I am writing, I am in the world, but not of it–preferring instead to engage in my private writing process.

Every one of us has had people in our lives who have made differences, who have changed us, who have disappointed us, who have made us feel exalted. The connection to these people, although they may not be in our lives presently, always lives within us. I believe that people appear on our paths when it is time. These people often serve as important signposts to signal change. Usually, the significance of their arrival can be understood years later after the important change or turning point has taken place.

DIRECTIONS

Close your eyes. I want you to think of a person in your life who has altered your path in some way. See this person clearly and fully before you. It may be that the person who appears before you was a childhood friend whom you may have forgotten about, or a current friend. What was her/his offering to you? Did you accept the gifts? What role did this person play in your life then? Now? How was your life altered?

When you are ready, open your eyes and draw on paper whatever image comes to mind when you think of this person. Don't worry if you don't actually depict this person as he/she looked. Just draw whatever comes to mind, what you remember as important. The drawing in this exercise, like the others in the book, serves merely as a catalyst for your writing.

Next to the picture, write down any specific words which come to mind when you think of the person. What was his/her gift to you? If you have a writing partner, introduce your friend to her. If you are writing alone, just proceed with the directions.

Take twenty minutes and write down all that comes to mind when you think about this person. Look at the picture. How has he/she made a difference in your life? How has he/she changed you? What do you recall? What have you forgotten? What do you need to remember?

You may be surprised at the information on the page when you are finished writing. Many women have told me that they have written about people that they hadn't thought about in years. These "forgotten" people are often responsible for the most pivotal changes in our lives.

Remember that you needn't write about a person that you know. One of the women in my workshop wrote about an author who changed her life. She never met the author, who was deceased, but her books profoundly influenced the way that this woman led her life. Always feel free to write what is truth in your life and never feel that you "have to" write about anyone in particular.

WOMEN'S VOICES

We drove across the bridge and the sun was out, nice and warm on my face and body. Your name came up and I wanted to cry. I quickly took a deep breath and calmed myself as the tears, already filling my eyes, slowly diminished. We talked about your goodness and how you deserved so much more in your life. I told him how loving and giving you had always been towards me, and that you were "too nice" sometimes for your own good. I think you deserve so much more quality in your life, but you say you are happy. I think you deserve a man in your life who will carry his own share of the responsibility. I think you deserve to be pampered, held up, cared for, nurtured. Perhaps you get all of these needs met in this relationship you now have. Perhaps I don't know what's best for you. I do know that I hurt when I think of how difficult your circumstances are right now and I know what that feels like. Perhaps you're not in touch with those feelings and don't feel any pain. Perhaps I am the one feeling the pain for you because you are not yet able. I pray you will feel the pain although I don't want you to feel the pain. But, in the pain will come the realization that you (in my view at least) are not being true to your own nature, to your best self, to your own preservation. In my perception of things, you are, as you always have, taking care of someone else rather than taking care of yourself; sacrificing your needs to those of another; losing yourself in another's problems; being that person's salvation and hope. I pray you can hold on long enough to feel the pain and then make the decision to love yourself instead of loving someone else.

–Mary Ellen Rescigno

*   *   *

Good friends are my most treasured possession. Like fine silver or gold, the friendships develop a warm patina as they grow and deepen with age. The comfort of a friend, someone who cares for you even when you are a real ass, is beyond value.

Those friendships built years ago and far away, that can be picked up again, almost mid-sentence without missing a beat. It's like having a box of clothes in storage and when you take the box out again, your favorite sweater still fits.

The ease of familiarity, the knowledge that you don't have to start fresh every time, that you don't have to make a good impression. Not to imply that you get to be lazy or abuse the friendship, or take the people for granted (well, maybe just a little). Eventually that would kill a friendship. But to know you don't have to sell yourself all the time or pretend to be someone you're not. That you are accepted; what a sense of reassurance.

The giving of friendship is altogether as precious as receiving it. To know someone well enough to treat them to something that they will always treasure; to know and appreciate their quirks and idiosyncracies, even to be able to tease them. To be admitted to their inner self, to give and to support, to make a difference to them, is a gift.

–Jeanne Dorward

* * *

Cousin Cecil lived in Riverside. She was just right for the neighborhood, she fit it to a tee, for it was old and ornate like her.

She could be seen any Sunday, walking down the old cobblestone streets, wearing her fine silk dress, and a hat with real feathers. She wore bracelets, necklaces, rings, and perfume. Her cheeks were red as beets with the rouge she wore, and the bright red lipstick surrounding her mouth made her look a little bit like a clown.

She was happy and sad all at once.

On some Sundays, we would find her sitting in the white gazebo, in the large green park across the street from the Temple.

At the sound of the last bell, we'd be out the door, across the street, and into the park, running for all we were worth towards the gazebo.

It was usually hot then. She seemed to be there mostly when it was hot. We'd find her sitting on a bench, perspiring just a little and fanning herself with a lovely pink fan.

"Come sit here beside me," she'd say, smiling, not missing a beat with the fan, and patting both sides of the bench. And we'd scamper up, fighting a little about who could sit next to her because there were three of us and that meant that one of us had to sit further away.

"My TV's on the blink," she'd say out of nowhere. "Color's not right. On my favorite show they all look green." We knew her favorite show was the one about the circus. Each week someone in the circus got killed and it would take the police along with the circus crew the whole hour to find out who did it.

"Maybe Daddy could fix it," I'd say, looking up at her. "Daddy could fix the TV." Then she would tell me I'm sweet and to prove it she'd fold me in her arms so that for a few minutes I'd be pressed up against her beautiful dress, surrounded by her soft, flabby flesh, and her strong perfume.

–Rebecca Geiger

* * *

Pick a number! Any number, honey, I feel lucky tonight . . . My Aunt Margie was a gambler who lived with us at intervals when she would not or could not pay her debts. I respected and adored her simply because she scorned people who worked for a living, my parents included. She wore granny-apple green negligees in the afternoon and when I went to bed at night, I pretended the negligees were mine.

Making a bet was the primary motivation that drove Margaret Silvestri out of her government-subsidized apartment. When it was necessary to eat, food was delivered by Frank's Deli, mainly because Frank had a crush on Margie and would let her pay with a check and duly exposed cleavage. Dirty clothes could be washed in the sink. A ten-inch black and white TV provided ample entertainment.

There were no friends or lovers, though, "Romance," she told me, "could only be found at the racetrack." Horses were beautiful. Horses were handsome and delicate, like dancers. Smoke, cheap beer, and wine infused the air until it became intoxicating; she couldn't breathe anywhere else.

By the time I reached the proud age of nine, my aunt and I understood each other. Translations were not necessary. I knew that when she said, "I'm taking a trip," she was really on her way to a Bingo game at a nearby Indian reservation. If Margie won a game or two she came home radiant and her left breast would appear much larger than her right. Sometime during my murky teen years, I finally realized where she was stuffing her prize money.

–Sandra Stevens

* * *

If only i could give myself to
(for the first time in my life i do not feel alone)

You, the color and
the smell and the shape of hope
and i want you (if you only knew)
how often I wonder
where were you
before the phone would ring
into my veins and i know
it is you
not a salesman, not my mother
Not an acquaintance calling to
discuss the 10:00 news because
when the phone rings sweetly
into my veins i know
your voice will hold me down
then pick me up carefully so
i won't fall and the cadence
of your words is like the ocean
pushing softly and (even though
i have only known you a short time)
every memory of you
puts another star in my sky
and a path of love unravels
in the darkness
when i think of how
you took my hand that first night
and somewhere i knew
Prayers were being pulled
out of suitcases (and if only
i could give myself to you)
and now when i sit at my desk
i feel i have more to say
and when politicians lie
it no longer matters
because i can rest my head on your chest
and you inspire me

—Sandra Stevens

* * *

Sherri Palladini
was one of the Gucci Girls
at the Academy and her last name
didn't really end with an "i."

Every day she wore
dozens of accessories
to complement a uniform that
could only flaunt the label of our Lord.

(a girl got to be a Gucci
by thinking thin,
applying professional make-up
in her New Car,
and by having a library of Gucci handbags)

In ninth grade
Sherri was engaged to Tony,
a Jesuit senior
who we all thought looked like Mussolini.

Once, during Health,
Sherri cried so profusely
she was sent home screaming
CATHOLICS WANT BABIES NOT BIRTH CONTROL!

Sometimes I wonder.
Where are you now, Gucci girl?

                                    –Sandra Stevens

*   *   *

Ever since I was a little kid I've done this really evil thing with
my toes. Well, not hurtful or mean evil–but weird, strange evil.

I have this unconscious habit of crossing my toes domino style,
one toe over the other. It's not intentional, but I find myself doing it
when I'm writing or reading, or talking on the phone. I'll look down
and notice that my toes are twisted and toppled over one another
like frightened little lemmings trying to leap off my feet.

This ability, this disorder, this genius, might not bother me so
much had I not seen toes exactly like mine on the foot of a very

unhappy person. These were not pretty toes, but horribly mangled, pained toes on a foot that seemed taller than it was wide. They belonged to the feet of my grandmother, Frida.

Frida was a nervous 85-pound dangle of a woman whose constant confidante was a burning cigarette which hung from her scarred, liver-spotted lips. The scar was from skin cancer that they apprehended years back. I was always amazed that such a wisp of a woman could get away with three packs a day and never incur anything more than a little spot of cancer on her lips.

Of course, 80 years had taken their toll on Frida, though there was still an odd strength about her as she heaved her tiny frame around the city on errands and doctors appointments–thanks in part to tall shots of bourbon first thing in the morning. But, generally her body had become a soft pack of bones and there was something stitched and patched together about her, making her look like an old faded doll.

Her dyed brown hair was thin like a child's and brushed strategically over her aging scalp. Her lipstick, an uncommon orangey shade often looked smeared because of her lip scar and seemed to tug the orange past her lips towards her nose.

But, the thing that made her look the strangest to me were her shoes. Frida had money for whatever she wanted, but because of the abstraction of her feet, she had to wear these clink, ugly orthopedic shoes for feet that were taller than they were wide. These shoes made Frida look cheap.

I've heard it said that old people tend to die after big holidays or big birthdays because they feel a sense of completion, having seen their families for the last time. But, I never got that sense from Frida. There was never a right time for anything and nothing was ever good enough for her.

At her 80th birthday party, I'd asked her how she was feeling and she said, "Lamby, sometimes I just feel like ssssllllllltttt," and gestured with her hand a slashing motion across her neck.

"Mama Frida wants to cut her throat," I mentioned casually to my boyfriend later. It wasn't unusual for her to complain like that; being alive seemed an awful burden for her, and not a day went by when she wouldn't remind you of it.

Frida told me of her life growing up in Salt Lake City. Her family had been one of the few Jewish families there and this adds to my picture of her home; very Germanic and proper, dark, lots of linen doilies, and very quiet. Her father, Amel, was stern, and her mother, Trixi, smoked cigarettes–unnerving the then non-smoking Frida who would dash about the house pulling curtains closed.

My grandfather, Francis, appeared on the scene as a traveling salesman for "Best Foods." He was some real playboy with his shiny, purple convertible Kissel car, double-breasted suit and hat. He came through town, met "the prettiest Jewish girl he'd ever seen" and asked Frida to marry him not three weeks later.

Frida agreed. They left for a life in California, and from that day on she wanted for nothing. There were beautiful clothes, large homes, upstairs and downstairs maids and chauffeurs. The three trips around the world filled thirteen leather bound photo books.

As a child, my mother remembers Frida weeping every night at the dinner table over a million things around her; dirty fingernails, dirtied clothes, drapes that weren't drawn, food that wasn't hot enough or my grandfather making everyone laugh at the table by putting the placemat on his head.

Frida even had a chance to fix her toes once, but when my grandfather found out the surgery would keep her off her feet for eight weeks, he refused to pay for it because he couldn't imagine running a house without her.

Frida went along with all of the decisions. If Papa didn't want to go out then she didn't go out. He was bored by ballets and concerts, so that was out too. During these nightly weeps, she'd cry, "And you won't even take me to a movie!" But, she never considered going alone or with a friend. Instead, she'd retreat to her bourbon and cigarettes.

The neighbors were the ones to find her and it was not nice. Everybody in the family thought it was suicide–at least at first.

But when I saw the car in the pool as it sat there, sunk, nose down, and when I saw for days afterwards, the murky layer of oil and gasoline that floated the surface of the water and oozed up through the grass around the pool, I had to remember if Mama Frida could have really driven her car into the swimming pool and deliberately drowned herself on that stormy, drenched afternoon in Los Angeles. The idea itself would have horrified her. Even the coroner said it was an accident, and he should know: there are a lot more effective, painless ways to do it.

We were all stunned. There had been four people in the house at the time of her plunge–my grandfather, his nurse, the cook, and the housekeeper–and not one of them had heard her go in. When the police descended upon the house and made for the pool, nobody realized that she was inside the car until the cook started running in circles around the edge of the pool, pointing and shrieking, "She in there! She in there!"

When I got the call from my father that night I couldn't help but feel that Frida had been moving toward that pool her whole life. And that this one act was the most defiant action she'd ever taken in a passive life full of new dresses, cigarettes, and doctor's appointments. "Way to go, Frida." I thought. "Didn't even give the old man a chance to say no."

The day she died it had been raining hard and by mid-morning she was in a fight with my grandfather over what would be served at dinner. She was on her way out of the house to meet their accountant and my grandfather screamed, "Frida, don't you dare leave this house in this rain!" but she did, returning minutes later for her black sweater, triumphantly shouting to everyone, "I'm going to die in this sweater!" They didn't pay her much mind because she was always saying things like that.

A couple of weeks earlier, she had said to my grandfather's nurse, "Sometimes I get so frustrated that I just want to drive my car right into the ocean!"

A week after Frida's death, my mother had a dream. She's a little girl and she's standing by the edge of the pool looking down at her mother's car which is lying there at the bottom. She dives into the pool and sees her mother inside. She tries to open the car door but her mother wags a disapproving finger at her as if to say, "I don't want any help, now get a move on."

There's some ridiculous code that says dead bodies can't be moved until a coroner thumps three times to make sure the person is really dead, and only then can the body be moved. So after they pulled her out of the car, the police left my grandmother lying half naked by her poolside for five hours in the rain while the hospital tried to find the coroner.

My parents, brother and sisters took turns sitting with her. They covered her with a blanket and were stroking her hair, talking to her, holding up an umbrella between them.

Five hours is a long time. Sometimes when the rain got really bad, they would to into the house for a while and she'd be left there in the rain as the flooding pool water washed over her. I keep wishing that I could have been there with her at the pool to stroke her head and keep her safe; something that I had never been able to do when she was alive.

They cremated her body on a gloomy, grey day and weeks later my family took her ashes out to sea on my grandfather's boat, The Misbehave. Frida had finally gotten her wish; she'd made it to the sea. "Be careful what you wish for," I'd told my sister remembering what the nurse had told me, "We're all a lot more powerful than we know."

–Laurie Marks

*   *   *

Forgive us our trespasses as we forgive those
As we forgive those

Two years and I still won't think of you
Can't talk about you
The sound of your name stains the air with bad omens

I learned it's Christian to forgive so I swallowed you,
pushed you out and froze you down
But

I am a river, the ice floes are melting and one day,
open mouthed, I'll pour myself out
I'll send myself across the Atlantic and you,
You'll be drowned.

Even now, you're drowning
Never mind, I've made a map to remember you
Visions of Unspeakable
Cowering in the closet, crawling ragged across the carpet

Leading me always to your beautiful hands,

Knew how to make a circle around my neck
Soft skin, felt like a caress until you started to squeeze
I have felt the thrill of suffocation, drifting into Forget

I still remember the rush of blue stars

As we forgive those who trespass against us
Forgive those who trespass

Crippled by the dark, you always had your way with me
Still have tubes of red lipstick you wouldn't let me wear

But I saw the look on your face when you knew I
was leaving you for the last time
Animal eyes, foot caught in the trap
(You knew the game was up)

Stretched into being, I took a deep breath without you
Blessed rain of pure oxygen

I remember you
Think now and then of how I once loved you so

Forgive us

–Christina Manning

*   *   *

Model Citizen, keeper of the flame
Liberty burns bright for men like you
Shining teeth, carrying the torch for a
new generation of Americans and all that

Fiscal hero, you stayed in your tax bracket
Ever true to some unchanging mark
But I could never find you

Mostly I remember that you split me wide open,
that your eyes were very blue

You wore silk ties, every woman's dream
In the vision I have of you, you were a
mindbender of a nightmare, with your erotic
mixups and mean misgivings

With your erotic mixups

Upright bolt, I wake in a sweating scream
You weren't so scared after all
And I'm nobody's baby now

–Christina Manning

*   *   *

What if I just faced this character? The dullness, deadness I feel. The extreme of the passive, lethargic, lacking direction person I have had to deal with or have not dealt with all my life. Outside on this October night, the sky, the lightest shade of mauve, the tree shapes now black, the crickets remind me that time is passing. The moon is halfway to fullness. I feel more than halfway to emptiness. The life and vibrance of the twins, their tenderness, touches me, nourishes me and marks the contrast. I feel life when I am with them. Kate so strong, full of energy–purpose with her job, ongoing plans. And when I return home, there's Caroline with her two–Gavin and Vivian, five years old and fourteen months, all full of enthusiasm with the project of clearing the yard, pruning trees, restoring the once magnificent property. I feel no sense of purpose today. I wonder what it would be like and I thought about this earlier today too–to surrender to this person, that is in listening to what she needs and wants. She is definitely a part of me that is coming right up to the surface–out of the depths. I want a voice too. This is the only way I can get your attention. You have had so many other distractions–no–you get busy and create distractions so you will not have to listen to this dull, quiet, lethargic person. You are caring for the twins–you must be fully present with them in all their moods. What is so different about me? This quiet child that wants to disappear into the background. I need your love and gentle nourish-ment–most of all your acceptance of me as a part of you. I can only change if I am fully accepted just the way I am. I can be nourished by your stillness, your wanting to be with me 100%. Responding to what I need–I simply ask that you know me. Not try to escape from me like I was an unwanted child. This person you see in your lover and want to be different. The key is unconditional love . . . Of your whole being of which I am a part.

–Jyoti Haney

Be not ashamed woman, you are the gates of the body and you are the gates of the soul.

–Walt Whitman, *Leaves of Grass*
(New York, Norton, 1968).

Chapter Ten

Reclaiming Our Feminine Bodies: Body Image

Our loathing of our bodies and our inability to accept them as part of us, our ache to banish our bodies, to cut fat, to lessen the wrinkles, to disassemble, and to disassociate ourselves from our own image is an illness in our culture.

Our self-hatred for our bodies, women's bodies, female bodies, is pervasive and begins when we are young. I listen to my friends share mutual discomfort with their bodies' "imperfections." I chime in about my own personal frustrations with my body. Although I am tall, slim, and healthy, I carry within me an outdated body image. This image comes from an adolescent's doubting eyes, a time when I felt awkward and afraid of my own body's power.

Women choose various vehicles for abandoning or embracing their bodies. Starvation diets, exercise, or drugs all force us into or out of our bodies. Menstruation, or the lack of it, serves as a potent reminder that we are feminine, we are women: fleshy, round, full, and alive. I think that childbirth and sex are probably the most profound and exquisite opportunities for a women to be totally present in her body. The nine-month process of carrying a child forces each woman to be aware of her body as her child grows within her. The lush and tactile pleasures of the senses that accompany love-making also provide a woman with the opportunity to experience her power, her pleasure, her self.

Since I reside in my head so much of the time, I have found that working out and dancing are the perfect vehicles for me to be in touch with my body. Certainly, studying dance therapy in graduate school in the early 1970s opened the door to my awareness of my own body/mind split.

I still cringe at my own despair about parts of my body and I hope that someday I can make peace. I am feminine; I have flesh. When I am filled with anger at my body, I try to remember a lover's gentle whispers reminding me how beautiful I was to him.

I wonder if we will ever have a generation of girl children, women-to-be, who won't know the definition of a diet; who will celebrate their bodies instead of starving them or gorging them to death. I wonder if this generation of healthy, accepting young women can take pride in their bodies, in their feminine images and can dwell inside of their bodies in comfort? Can we live in a time when anoretic adolescents are not the models for what a woman should look like? When hips full, tummy puffy, breasts large, and bodies full of flesh can be inhabited with grace? Can we rejoice in the amazing configuration of the feminine body: full, fat, thin, bony, and uneven? This is the truth of what "real women's" bodies look like.

Can a new generation of women try on bathing suits each summer without mentioning their hatred of a body part? Can women pass on the love, trust, and inner rejoicing about their bodies to their daughters? Can we refuse to submit to unauthentic demands to look or dress in inappropriate ways?

A breast enhancement, a tummy tuck, a face lift, are all viable options for any woman when *she* chooses them, but the statistics of women who engage in plastic surgery in the 1990s are increasing. The number of teenagers who have plastic surgery "to correct themselves" is frightening. I am disgusted when I peruse the ads in women's magazines and see gaunt, spiritless, empty young models peering out at me.

Whenever I led a writing workshop on body image with women, I was always struck and startled by the fact that although each group possessed its own collection of young and old women, fat and thin women, black, white, and brown women, *not one* woman attending ever admitted that she was happy with her own body. Rooms full of intelligent, talented, creative, and beautiful women were unable to accept their bodies.

I cannot promise that these exercises will change the way you feel about your body, but I do know these exercises can provide greater understanding in the ways in which you see your feminine body.

DIRECTIONS

Take out a sheet of paper and draw your perfect body. Draw this body as you would like it to be. When you are finished, take out a sheet of paper and on one side list all of the things you like about your appearance, your body, and the image you project. On the other side, list all of the things you dislike about your body. (Your appearance and the image you project.)

When you are finished, if you have a partner to work with, show her your "ideal body." Just share the information without comment. After you have shown her your picture, read from both your lists, for both the positive and the negative attributes. Feel free to speak about how you see the other person, *if* they would like that feedback. *Ask* them what they would like.

After you are finished with the exercise, go through the list of negative attributes and next to each attribute, label what is *true* as you know it and what is *false*. When you are finished, look at the list and pay attention. Was any of this negative information told to you from a family member? A lover? A relative? A stranger? If you can remember, write down the exact age you were when you received these myths about your body.

Look at your list again. Select one aspect of your body that you listed negatively and look at the name of the person who gave you that negative information about your body. Write to them directly for twenty minutes, in a letter form if you like, and let them know their negative messages have affected you. Tell them what you believe, and how you felt, hearing their denunciation of your body. When you are finished with the letter, crumple it up and burn it.

Frequently, the core of our hatred for our bodies comes from the outside, from thoughtless, cruel, and unkind people. This is not the truth about our bodies, about *your* body, and you don't have to accept their information as your truth.

DIRECTIONS

Close your eyes and picture yourself in a comfortable setting. Clear your mind and be ready to meet someone who can offer you important information about your body. You may see the appearance of a symbol, a person, or sense a presence. Listen and accept what happens.

When you are finished, write down all that you remember. Note what happened during your visualization. What information about your body was offered to you? How did you feel about hearing this information?

Now, I would like you to write yourself a love letter, a real love letter. Write yourself the kind of letter that you would like to receive from someone who truly loved you. Give yourself permission to write what you really want to hear. Keep in mind that *no one* will read this letter.

Put the letter in an envelope and address it to yourself. Exchange the envelope with your writing partner, or, if you are working alone, ask a friend to mail it to you in the next three weeks. You don't have to explain the contents, just ask if they will do it. If you feel awkward about mailing it, put the envelope in a place that you usually do not visit so you can happen upon it in the future.

WOMEN'S VOICES

I have the Kreiss family hips–generations of Hungarian peasant farmers on my mother's side. I've seen old photos, Great-Grandmother Malvina, Grandma Julia, Great Aunt Helen. There they are– there *we* are–all of us pear-shaped (to be polite), our bodies forged for child-bearing.

The bodies of my relatives, however, have a rootedness mine lacks, like tree trunks merging with the earth. Perhaps it's just the black and white photograph that lends them such gravity, gives their legs such weight, their hips such solidity.

Perhaps it's just that I know they were farmers–they raised chickens–and the apron stretching across Malvina's broad thighs means fecundity to me, imparts an earthiness I have no claim to.

They are beautiful, somehow, in a way I have never felt.

I've joked about these peasant hips, my baby-making body. I can touch up my eyes with make-up, my cheeks with blush, I can prop or pump or push up my breasts, but I've had, I'll *have*, these hips for life.

For life.

Perhaps that's exactly what those women in the photograph are telling me, all my big-hipped Kreiss relations. Maybe *that* is their legacy, not jewels or furs or words of wisdom, but this body I've spent years trying to alter–and the life, and history that they have passed onto me, and that–for good for bad–I'll one day pass on to another Kreiss daughter.

We are bound, tied, connected, created, molded in the same form. *(Same damned hips.)* Generation after generation. For life.

–Susan Karp

* * *

Last night, I took down the still-soft clay from M.C.'s workshop. The half-born images I had shaped that day rested surprisingly together in a glorious glob (somehow I had expected them to disappear altogether.) Still wondering about the various images, I recalled Kamae's words as she sat beside me that afternoon. "Looks like a goddess keeps showing up." A few words and I have a little more permission, just enough to push myself that much closer to the creative edge. The clay is in my hands, shape-shifting herself into a female form. Definitely my hands . . . moving, gliding, grabbing, pinching, smoothing. Within seconds, head and shoulders emerge naturally. How can this be? I've never used clay before! Artistically, this is my most creative moment; all these months of hearing about the divine connection within the unconscious, now coming into being. I know now the godlike feeling of creating woman. The clay woman and I become one. As I detach a clay breast, a flood of shock enters my body and I cry out in apology, "Oh, poor clay! That's how my mother must have felt." So my woman body still holds the memory of my mother's horror; her breast no longer a source of life, is sliced away. Now one gone, then the other.

–Suzanne Chaumont

* * *

A crocus just a moment in life
Alive amidst the chill of snow
Life seems above the unseeminglessness
of winter, the raw blanket.

A baby just a moment in my body
Alive within the tangle of chromosomes
Life felt against the relentlessness
Of death: the bloody products of conception.

The piece of me alive then dead
Two heartbeats again become one
Two bodies separate forever
The souls entwined, spirits together.

The peace of years and time
A gift of tears and knowing
To be grateful for agony and wrenching
And know the truth pain offers.

–Zoe Smith

*   *   *

I had been born with odd-shaped eyes. My parents worried that I might be cross-eyed. They took me to many eye specialists who all said that I was *not* cross-eyed and that the shape of my eyes would change and improve as I grew older. I still have unusual eyes and have often been asked if I am Oriental. Also at that time my mother felt I needed braces on my feet and legs to correct a slight pronation of my feet. The problems did not affect my ability to walk or the way I looked, yet she felt it needed to be corrected.

The message I received from my mother's worries about my eyes and feet was that I was defective, faulty, not good enough. This feeling of inferiority was compounded by my sister's arrival because as fate would have it, she was born "perfect." Blonde, blue-eyes, petite, dainty, and fragile–these words describe my baby sister. All the family friends raved about the arrival of the "Little Princess," the "Swedish Bombshell." I was most definitely mad with jealousy, and deeply hurt. Not only had I been dethroned from my position as baby in the family, I had been replaced by someone better suited, in my parent's eyes, for the role.

–Shelly Compton

* * *

In my twenties, it was in my body.
I was attracted to a variety of men.
I talked with my body.
The clothes I chose, the perfume I wore,
A song, a scent could arouse me–calling up images of
days and nights of spinning, whirling in love.
All my pores were open, all my senses waiting to collide . . .
I bought flowers, candles, and books.

In my thirties, my passion was still in my body.
I felt more sensual. My husband's voice, a passing
glance from his friend could arouse my senses. I became
more intimate with my husband. I learned to listen
and to touch. When I spoke, I began to use my hands.
I bought perfume, bottles of petit sarahs, and books.

Now, in my forties, I don't know where my passion lies.
Buried somewhere under layers of skin. I think the
years are slowly swallowing me up, dimming my senses,
clogging my pores. I take care of my body but I don't
polish it or decorate it as in years past. It is now
a vehicle, a means of getting me from one place to
another. My expectations of it are simple: don't break
down; start up each morning without too much of a fuss.
I still buy books.

–Joyce Roschinger

* * *

T and A. It all comes down to tits and ass. But I suppose mainly tits. This is the part of my body I have always been most self-conscious about.

When I was a girl, I would study the bodies in my father's *Playboy* magazines, looking for signs and clues to my distant self. My sister is three years older than me, and I watched her too, calmly noting that she had it all: breasts, hips, the quintessential hourglass figure.

At 13, shirtless, I would stand before the mirror studying my chest. My friends and sisters would stand there too, all in a row, shirtless before the mirror comparing our breasts.

Thirteen went by, then 14-15 loomed. But no change. My breasts remained frighteningly small. I thought of mail-ordering. You know, those enlargement kits advertised in the backs of comic books. I would sit in the hallway, comic book in hand, dreaming of how I would order a kit. It would come in a brown paper package, and no one would know, not my parents, my sisters or friends. If I did the exercises diligently, in no time, I'd go from a size 32 to a size 36. But, it was impossible, really, seeing that I had no money, and surely someone would get to the mail before I would.

–Rebecca Geiger

*   *   *

I'm telling!

Ruthie, are you storying again?
You're just a tattle-tale, a yellow-bellied, lying,
fraidy-cat stool pigeon. A Girl.

I was four, the first time I was flat on my back under a boy.
Under a house on damp earth with cobwebs and black widow
spiders, he rode me the way he'd seen his father ride his mother.
I clearly recall my thoughts: I was bored. It felt like a replay
of a part of my past, though not from this life.

When I was seven, the little boy next door wanted to see me dance
naked for him in the closet. I did, but I thought, "What for?"
We had both seen Susan Hayward perform for Ruham Bey in
Ali Baba and the Forty Thieves, and I knew I was an
inadequate substitute. Couldn't he see the difference?

I was 14 when my brother's best friend fell in love with me.
I broke if off finally, telling him I didn't feel the same
way about him, that it was dishonest to pretend. Neither of
those boys comprehended my lack of ardor, or my need to play
fair.

At 17, I tried to dump my boyfriend. Later on, our married life was a continuation of his pursuit of sex–with me, with others–a quarter of a century of it until I ended it by divorce.

For 60 years, from the time I was under the house, rape has been my experience of femaleness: Forced entry, visual rape, marital demands and betrayal. I've actually heard the expression that, "if a raped woman enjoys the experience, then it's not rape." Enjoyment of rape is inconceivable to me.

I'm taking the stand as a reliable witness: Until the expectation changes that females of all ages are to submit without objection; until the words spoken by a female are heard as real words; until female-girls-women utter those words– without apology, with conviction, with assurance, then four-year-olds will continue to lie on their backs under houses, being ridden by little boys, and feel as if it feels familiar, from past lives and on into our futures without end.

–Ruth Hynds

*   *   *

Flabby white, with scattered red mole-like dots inherited from my mother. Viewed from the side, it sticks out farther than my breasts–almost a third appendage. I stuff it into control-top panty-hose. I suck it in and pull my belt one notch tighter. I take a deep breath and zip up my size 10 Banana Republic jeans to hold it in. I wake in the morning, tumble naked out of bed and, the first person I see in the full-length mirror is the one with the *belly*, pooching out from a narrow waist (even that begins to be flabby at the sides). Some mornings–right there–I will bend over and do 20 yoga belly lifts and think, "If I would just do this every morning, I would have a flat, model-like tummy in 30 days or less."

Thirty-three years ago, when I was pregnant with my son, what a relief it was not to wear the girdle and nylons. I could finally let go–let it just relax and be a belly. It's all right to be pregnant and have a belly. Then, I loved feeling the skin grow tight and glisten silky as the life pushed forward month by month. I loved my popped-out navel–finally able to see and to be seen. This was the *belly* expressing itself to its fullest–no constraints by clothes or judgments.

Why not know and love this Belly as if it were always with child, accept this gentle mound as part of me? Let it jiggle and bounce, let it Be? All those models with board-flat bellies and vacuous faces with shallow smiles–why do I feel there is something there to emulate?

–Jyoti Haney

*   *   *

My breasts used to be a size 34A; never large enough for my husband. He wanted me to get a boob job: "If you really loved me, this would be something you would whole-heartedly agree to . . . . " Well, there were so many other things he wanted from me, luckily this didn't remain the focus for very long.

After the divorce, my breasts rounded and firmed to a 36B. I tossed out the push-up bras and padded bikini tops and replaced them with natural contour bras and body suits. I now even had cleavage!

I love lying between my peach-colored sheets, cupping my breasts in my hands. I love the response of my nipples to my touch–the sensual rippling that starts there and electrifies all of my self. I remember a dream of my breasts filled with milk, dripping into the mouths of waiting babies, as a mother bird feeding her young. I think of my own two children–grown now. I did not nurse them because it was "out of style" back then. When I see mothers suckling their young with a deep contentment in their eyes, I know something of that joy–as in now through the gentle nourishment of myself caressing these soft round orbs.

–Jyoti Haney

But I always recognize the forces that will shape my life. I let them do their work. Sometimes they tear through my life like a hurricane. Sometimes they simply shift the ground under me, so that I stand on different earth, and something or someone has been swallowed up. I steady myself, in the earthquake. I lie down, and let the hurricane pass over me. I never fight. Afterwards I look around me, and I say, "Ah, so this at least is left for me. And that dear person has also survived."

–Josephine Hart, *Damage*
(New York, Alfred Knopf, 1991, pg. 173).

Chapter Eleven

Passages in a Woman's Life

The process of life forces us to bend, to meld, to accommodate. Often, we fight these transitions in our lives and kick and scream. We lie frozen at the idea of altering our paths in any shape. Some women, wise women, greet these changes with open arms, for they know that these times are inordinately powerful and offer a woman the greatest opportunity for growth and understanding.

The changes that I am referring to take us out of our pasts and plunge us headlong into a new reality. An adolescent girl is on the brink of womanhood, a young teen has a child, a woman leaves her husband of forty-five years, while another declares her love for a female lover. I believe that the power of our passages lies in the internal transformation itself. I am referring to that not quite developed time in-between, that murky time which cannot be defined. This shifting occurs while we are in the shedding stages of "what we were" to "what we will become." This emotional shedding not only transforms us physically but emotionally as well. Our consciousness changes, our energy changes, our thoughts change; and, although we may desire it, there is no turning back once the transformation is initiated.

When we leave our safe havens to embrace the unknown, and depart into what can only be described as "the unknowable," it is always both stimulating and frightening. When a woman leaves her husband, she embarks on a whole new world without her "other," with only herself to count on. When a woman experiences menopause, she experiences her physical and emotional body in a completely different manner.

I am most interested in the internal transformation process which accompanies the major shifts in our lives. This area interests me the most because I have re-created myself many times. I have moved cross-country three times and set up my world in Boston, New York, and San Francisco. I have had many lovers, innumerable jobs, countless friends, and I have suffered the anguish that some of my passages have brought to me.

The internal transformation which takes place during these transitions are profoundly individual. We all bleed for the first time, make love for the first time, choose lovers, leave lovers, change jobs, lose family members and in some cases, have children. These are all important passages in a woman's life, however, it is how a woman experiences the internal metamorphosis that really counts.

Many of our passages are never spoken of, and as a result, they create isolation, frustration, and confusion for many women. We think that "we are supposed to feel" a certain way and when our internal world is in conflict with these ideas, we suffer. The fear, the strangeness of the new, and the acceptance of the inner changes do not have to be painful. Some women become depressed, others use alcohol and drugs to quell the pain.

Sadly, our culture does not applaud our passages. We don't usually speak about our sexual transformations or our disappointments. We try to cover up our frustrations and failures and shove them deep down into the darkness.

Judith Duerk's wonderful book, *Circle of Stones: Woman's Journey to Herself*, (Luramedia Books), is a wonderful and inspirational book for women. She asks, "What if woman were to allow herself to trust her own unhappiness and make life changes–What if a woman trusted her own tears enough to listen to them, to make real changes . . . . What if she trusted her anger, her irritation, her illness, even her depression, as signs that her own life was calling to her?"

I love her use of language and her ideas. What would your world look like if you knew that no matter how challenging, exhilarating, scary, or exciting the passages that you were experiencing would be, you knew in your heart that you could find and seek out the company of women who could guide you?

I encourage you to share your stories of safe passage with other women in your life. Speak of your fears, your triumphs, your descent. Let the younger women hear the stories from the elders, let the elders hear from the young.

Embrace your internal transformation and know that you are carrying on the same process that has existed for other women before you. When you do the writing exercises in this chapter, invite other women in your friendship circles to join you. Learn from each other and most important, listen.

DIRECTIONS

Take out a piece of paper and many colored pens, crayons, or pencils. On this sheet of paper, I want you to visually document the important passages that you have made as a woman. Create a visual road map of where you have come from and where you are going. Don't worry about how to do this; whatever comes to mind as your first thought is usually the best. You may want to document only the turning points in your life, or create a geographical rendering of where you have lived. Some women choose to illustrate the highs and the lows of their internal worlds, while others list lovers as a demarcation of their romantic journey. What matters is that *you* choose how you want to document your life.

Take twenty minutes and draw the passages in your life. When you are finished, show the map to the others, or merely look at it yourself. These exercises are wonderful vehicles for documenting your autobiography in an unorthodox manner and frequently offer a great deal of information.

When you are finished looking at the visual road map that you have created, I want you to choose one event on the map that you feel is particularly significant. Take out a sheet of paper and fill the page up with as much information as you think is important. You may want to include your age, where you lived, who you loved, whatever feels right to you. Close your eyes and try to remember all that you need to. Focus your mind like a movie camera, capturing all of the important moments, colors, and even conversations, if you remember them.

If you are having trouble with these exercises, start by writing about a time in your life when you truly felt "grown-up" by wearing or owning an article of clothing. It may be when you bought your first bra, smoked your first cigarette, bought tampons, or birth control. It doesn't matter what you choose since you are the only one who will know what is right for you. The wide range of writing that follows illustrates that point quite well.

WOMEN'S VOICES

I think of eyes. My own eyes, specifically. I see a low wall, brick or something, and two eyes looking over it. That's all I can see–the wall and the eyes; the wall, like one of those veils Iranian ladies wear, masking the rest of them, making it impossible to tell if they're laughing or not, so really you don't know what they're thinking. The wall was a good vantage point, from which I could see just what was happening. There wasn't a lot I could do though.

——————

Lately, I notice eyes. I don't know why, but I only notice blue eyes. Lately, I don't dream, but I notice eyes. The blue ones are telling me something.

——————

Thinking of my childhood, I think of pain. A blue pain maybe? I think of my sisters with joy, my mother with love, and my father with pain.

——————

I think in my house, there was a tension. A certain tension masked by normalcy. My father went to work every morning, going around the table to kiss each of us goodbye. He always carried a briefcase, inside of which was (among other things) a stethoscope, one of those flashlights that you stick in your ear, syringes, and various medications. He was a doctor.

It seems that on the surface, we were all very controlled, very good, but underneath, each of us was seething with a kind of anger, and a kind of pain. It was a blue pain, I think. It must have been.

–Rebecca Geiger

*   *   *

The little girl on the swing
with dimpled cheeks
and flowing curls;
Her shoes point to the sky
as she defies gravity.

Feeling powerful and free
she squeals, "I'm flying!"
pumping her heels to attain
a more daring elevation; then
realizes her limit with this
contraption.

For now she is pleased,
but dreams of soaring stuff her
imagination . . . "Maybe some day . . . ";
she blinks and sighs as her shoe tips
scrape the sand and dig in deep grooves.
Abruptly, she halts, heels locked in,
arms gripping metal chains on either side.

She rises and walks away
from the place that gave her magic
for a moment.

Left behind by the girl,
the swing gently moves in the still air
longing for a passenger.

–Mary Ellen Rescigno

*   *   *

My thirteenth birthday. My godmother, Aunt Joan, had sent a package from Oregon. We had all finished dinner and were sitting around the big oak table (with several leaves added). Grandparents (Mom and Pop), my two little brothers, Aunt Thelma and Uncle Bill, Teddie (my Aunt younger than me), my parents–Connie and Joe.

I don't remember any of the other gifts which I probably opened before this one came in the mail. It is in a brown wrapping, neatly tied with string, wound many times around and knotted to form a square for my name and address written in the meticulous manner of Aunt Joan: rounded capitals much larger than the other letters, with swirls at the end of each part of my name and the address. I felt important and a little uneasy. Her gifts were usually very practical. I needed scissors to cut the string around the thick brown paper (a carefully reused grocery bag). I reached in to find a delicate flowered paper package with a scarlet ribbon tied with a perfect double bow.

My two little brothers, one and three years old, are getting restless. Jan has wiggled out of his high chair and is running toward the kitchen. Joe is beginning to make wanting-attention sounds. I am distracted and then look up to see all the others still watching me, now opening the ends of the flowered paper. The gift is still concealed by more neatly wrapped tissue paper. I carefully fold the flowered paper (just as Aunt Joan would have done) and lay it aside. "Well, aren't we ever going to see what it is?" my great grandmother asks in her thick Austrian accent. She is drumming her fingers on the table. I wish everyone wasn't watching me. I would like to slide out of view under the table, taking the package with me. Aunt Joan has scotch taped it on both sides. Mom slits it open for me with a table knife and I take a deep breath, open it finally and there is now light pink tissue paper still hiding this "gift." Unfolding it, here is something of white shiny satin, with lace. I close my eyes tightly and pray that it isn't a bra. "Well, what is it?" Pop asked, his brown eyes smiling. I pull slowly up for full view a garter belt as laughter goes around the table. "I don't even know how to wear this thing!" I poke hopefully beneath the tissue to see what else might be there. I pull out two nylon stockings. I feel my face grow hot and hear Mom saying, "Well, I guess you're going to have to act like a lady now!"

-Jyoti Haney

*   *   *

Once, I heard Daddy hitting Mommy and I heard banging around in the kitchen. I was afraid and I was mad. How dare he hit my mother! But I didn't say anything out loud. Inside, I screamed at him and said, "I hate you. You big bully! You jerk!" He didn't hear me actively say this until I was about 12 years old. Then, I did tell him; and he hit me in the face and told me to "Shut up or I'll shut you up for good!" meaning, "I'll kill you." I didn't even care. I was so sick of him, I wasn't afraid anymore. I was willing to risk my own life just to prove a point. I must have been pretty brave and pretty smart to stand up to him. No one else would, except me.

One time, when I was 19, he hit me and couldn't stop. I just kept yelling back at him. I told him that everyone in the house was afraid of him and that he was pushing everyone away. I asked him, "Is that what you want?" I used the truth to hurt him and I felt very powerful. The more I talked, the more he hit me; but, I knew I was hurting him, so I became numb and I didn't feel anything when he hit me. I walked into the bathroom, but I didn't cry. Then, I went down into the playroom to iron. He'd hit me pretty hard in the face. I thought he'd broken my nose. He said he was sorry afterward, but I thought he was disgusting. I also felt sorry for him; but, when he said "I love you," I said to myself, "Funny way of showing it."

My mother came downstairs to see if I was OK and told me to just keep quiet or he would really hurt me. I felt sorry for her, but I was disgusted with her too. I said, "Maybe you have to put up with this, but I don't." I felt bad after saying this, but that's how I felt. I moved out shortly after.

–Mary Ellen Rescigno

*   *   *

I know I would miss San Francisco
if I moved somewhere *else*. If I became just another
woman pushing heavy shopping carts through the wide aisles
of identical merchandise.
Someday, I'd remember that street.
That street in a neighborhood.
That neighborhood in a city–where shopping
(among other things) was much more diverse.

If I lived in a city I could finally call home (if only
because I could afford it); A place where Betty Davis
movies belong to the past and backyards are more common
than parking tickets. A place where every action doesn't
have a political reaction. So that the next time a bulky

man in a pick-up truck decides to throw an egg my way, it
will be because he doesn't like my shoes or the color of my
hair, not because I'm walking on a certain street in a
certain city where "everyone knows what that means."

I know I'd miss San Francisco
the first time an embalmed librarian winked at me from the
grave after I asked where all of Henry Miller's books were
hidden. And, of course I wouldn't be able to savor a
vigorous cup of joe without going out of my way. Going out
of one's way in most cities involves getting into a car,
and I don't have one of those.

So forget the reasonable rents and the generic restaurants
with over-sized parking lots. As I write yet another
good-bye letter to the only city in America that I love, I
realize that I'm not going anywhere because I *hate* rows of
identical merchandise and I *love* Betty Davis movies and I
couldn't care less about bigots and pick-up trucks who come
into my neighborhood to bully me and my friends simply
because they're bored with their own sexuality.

Yes. The backyard will just have to wait.

–Sandra Stevens

   I always had the Bear. I would sleep with him, and hold him; and,
I think I used to bite his nose which was plastic and I thought it
tasted pretty good.
   He was pretty funky looking. His eyes were like clear buttons,
and I think he had a plastic tongue that stuck out a little. His fur
was well worn because he'd been around forever.
   So maybe he was the forever bear. I think I liked him for that
and also for the fact that he was little, like me. He seemed smart
actually. A little bear, but sharp.
   There was something comfortable and easy about him–I didn't
have to pretend with him because he already knew everything.
   Overall, I had this tremendous respect for him–he seemed to
know so much and, without a word, he carried it all around with
him.
   I think, for his seniority, I respected him more than any of the

other toys. It's funny that I've never thrown him away. I think he sits now in a box in my closet.

−Rebecca Geiger

*   *   *

If I knew when I was younger what I know now, my life would have been different. It's difficult to imagine the hypothetical: would my life have been different if there had been a place where I could have gone to be with women? I get cynical. But, I can imagine that my selves would have been better served−my self-esteem, self-respect, self-regard, had I known then what I know now. My sexuality would have been channeled differently with more self-respect and restraint. My body image would have been more polished−the dents accepted, the curves applauded. I would have seen my education from a different, more thoughtful perspective. My own talents would have been recognized, not stifled.

I'm not sure that being with women could have taught me a "quiet centeredness." Who would these teachers have been? Not the women I knew when I was a child. My mother and her friends certainly weren't enlightened until fairly recently. Could it be that wisdom comes with age and experience? My teachers, mostly women throughout elementary and junior high school, didn't seem that enlightened either. Had I the opportunity to have met Georgia O'Keefe or some such anomaly of the female sex of my childhood years, I could have been very different indeed, but it's all hypothetical. I believe that the rare individual−male or female−has the gift of some sort of perceived enlightenment, but many are probably hermits like O'Keefe, or phonies.

I suppose it would have been easier had I had a mentor who could have spared me some of the pain along the way by teaching me a "quiet centeredness" in my early days. Was it necessary that I endured social promotion in elementary school, date rape in college, an abortion that broke my heart, three divorces in one decade in the school of hard knocks in which human beings enroll at birth? Could a place to be with women have made my foresight 20-20? Could my mistakes, my lack of clarity and judgment have been avoided? The ultimate rationalization for pain in childhood is living through it and thereby gaining the opportunity to make it right later in life–growing–as a woman, as a person. And while this is now cliché, I can take the responsibility and the credit for feeling some degree of contentment in my lifetime.

–Cary Davis

*   *   *

I am in Greece, and experiencing things different from anything I had expected. But, expectations are damned on this trip.

I thought revelations and realizations would hit me like shock waves, yet they are occurring gradually–natural progressions–like things or ideas that I have always known on some level, yet have never admitted before.

Away from all my familiar supports, I am finding out more *what* I want than who I am. Perhaps the two go hand-in-hand.

Have I ever really confronted myself? *Myself*, underneath all the protective devices. There's a side of me that is always aware, hyper-aware of everything. It forms an edge to drunken nights, an edge knifely-sharp and ever-present. It prevents me from ever being *in* myself.

It seems I cannot get away from my mind, from my thoughts. And that edge is my distance. I do not live moments; I dissect them. I control the origins and the destinations–what a "willful will" I have.

I have been "aiming" all of my life. So what is me in the rawest sense?

Go beyond the surface. *Crumble*. Go into yourself. *Crumble*. Go into the black. *Crumble*. Continue. Continue.

Is there anything there? Is there any me there? Are you built on *nothing*?

I cannot leave until I figure that out.

I am three tunnels down, in the dark. I look at the water–I see black. I look into the hottest suns of Paros–I see black. I look into the eyes of shopkeepers–I see black.

I am the lowest point in myself I have ever been. I am ill. My mouth fills with a taste, an odor, a disease. I am *sick* of myself. I am very far from New York City.

And I'm a Phoenix. I see a . . . no, I don't *see* light. I *feel* it. It begins in my spine, and straightens my back. It rises through my rib cage, through my lungs.

It shines out of *my* eyes. Or not mine exactly.

I suddenly have a glimpse of the person I am destined to become. I am not her *yet*; I am not *that* Susan.

But God! I am powerful! More than that–I am limitless. I am replete in myself. (I am not *her* yet.)

Somehow three tunnels down in myself, continents away from home, oceans from New York City, I see me. I *am* me. I have been running from me all my life.

I am not lost. I am not black. I have not crumbled.

Everything is possible.

Right now, I am surrounded by all that I own–everything in my pack, my small bag; I am nothing more than what I have with me.

Will I spend tonight waiting for a boat with 21 Greek drachmas to my name?

What to do, what to do?

(There is always an alternative.)

–Susan Karp

* * *

I travel on the scent of lilac.

Back to springtime in Pennsylvania
when I was young and wild
and filled baskets with its storm-soaked boughs.
Enough lilac in my nose for a lifetime.

Back further to small backyards in Pittsburgh
when the sweet purple smell floated on the steelmill air
and announced Spring.

To childhood afternoons–escaping on the pink arch of bleeding hearts
and into the quiet crowd of lily-of-the-valley in my father's garden.
And the stolen fragrance of the next door neighbor's treasure.

There are a few lilac trees in California.
Spring comes here to seawashed slopes
ablaze with poppies in the gleaming grasses
beneath the aerial swoops of courting hawks and ravens.

So I travel on the scent of lilac.

–Kathleen Byrne

* * *

I have a hand on my shoulder now. It is encased in a dark blue velvet glove–heavy and soft.

I can feel the sensuous fabric brushing against my neck. I can sense the strength of the hand within. It is warm and calm and constant. The touch is light and changes from one breath to the next–one moment playful, then steadying, at another time it guides and reminds.

It isn't the bony hand of my mother, or the leaden weight of the religion I was forced to follow. Nor does it suddenly appear with a guilty push or a nagging nudge. Instead, it rests like sunlight and sends warmth to my heart. The velvet hand gives me a momentum forward to take that step, to breathe out and to reach for the next moment which will act as platform to the next.

The movement forward creates a soft breeze that caresses and teases. It rises up to blow away the dust of inertia and neglect. My sails are unfurled now–the torpor is shaken loose. The sob that has been caught in my throat breaks free and fills the air with a wonderful ringing yell. My heart leaps at the sound. Is that me?

Is that really me?

–Kathleen Byrne

* * *

Whenever I go back to Los Angeles I feel compelled to shave off half the hair on my body. It's an odd ritual which has something to do with certain transitions of age and spirit.

Recently, on one of these freshly shaven trips, I was at a party and ran into the man who had been my pediatrician as a child. Dr. Wile–the kindly old fellow who had administered shots, blood and luscious red lollipops for me for years.

Patient, wise, and sweet smelling. Dr. Wile, who had instructed me as a plump adolescent on the art of substituting bananas for butter on toast. "A fraction of the calories!" he marveled, "you'll love it."

I trusted this man, but I stuck to the butter. When my body ballooned in collegiate angst, weighed down by beer and bratwursts–a voice in my head kept chiming, "bananas, not butter!"

Dr. Wile never saw the result of this doughy blossoming. I was seeing grown-up people doctors by then, and my maladies were of a more mature nature. Ladylike. Secret. Disturbing. But the transition from lollipops and *Hi-Q* magazines to waiting rooms oozing with Jean Naté and *Good Housekeeping* was a mysterious metamorphosis which may be traced back to a single summer day in Dr. Wile's office.

"It's time!" I had cried to my mother one afternoon in July.

The next thing I knew, she and I were sitting in Dr. Wile's office facing the good doctor, who was stationed behind his fortress of a desk. One hand cradled a phone, but he motioned us to sit down as he returned to his conversation.

Here was the man who had poked dozens of needles into my bottom, and whose thumbs had thumped their way across the terrain of my back for sixteen years, cruising over soft bone, and dodging anxious pimples. I felt obscene for what was coming.

"Birth control," I said.

Dr. Wile sat there for a moment with an odd smile on his face kneading his hands silently summing up his present situation.

"Well now," he said in a friendly sort of way. Plenty of kids must have passed through his office over the years, leaving him when their bodies dictated those growing needs. But I felt like a traitor. It wasn't so much that I didn't need him anymore–in fact, I needed all the help I could get.

I was. . . naive. My body was like a runaway train. I once tried to halt it when I was twelve by shaving off the new sproutings between my legs. I had a "date" that night with a boy in the supermarket parking lot. I remember nervously taking the razor in hand and locking the bathroom door. For a moment I considered asking my mom if the hair was "normal" for a girl my age, but I knew she would suspect something. So I hacked away at it, my enemy, traitor–the thing that would give me away.

Coming to Dr. Wile now was par for the course. I was never ready for the things I let boys do to me in supermarket parking lots–and I wasn't ready for the birth control now. But it all seemed unavoidable.

I was trying to crawl out of the ditch of adolescence, and entering the sexual realm seemed about as far from home as I could get. It was my ticket out.

"Do you know what love is?" Wile asked, his brows forming a blockage across his eyes. I knew this was a trick question and I felt trapped. If I attempted to answer him he would try to make me think about what I was doing–and I couldn't let that happen. A flurry of color and sound sped through my head. I turned the mental volume up high so that I could see him, but not hear what he was saying.

I'd done this a lot with my dad when he was giving me tennis lessons. It used to infuriate me when he would stop our game to cross over to my side of the court to correct my swing. "This is how you swing the racket," he would say as he glided my arm through the air. "Nice and easy," he would croon. This drove me crazy and the only thing I could fight him with was the word *Psychedelic*. So as Dad took hold of my grip, I squeezed my eyes shut and screamed as loud as I could in my head that deafening, defiant word "*Psychedelic!*" oblivious to the man swinging my arm through the air.

So there, Dr. Wile was talking about Love–and hell, I just wanted to play the game.

I ended up getting the pills, though I think I left his office feeling treasonous and even abandoned by him.

When I ran into Wile recently, the scars and cuts from the rollercoaster years that followed weren't so visible, and he was spared the details of my travels since we had last met, eleven years before.

I felt like I had come clean of those more reckless times. I was still a curious person, but I didn't feel the need to explore the underbelly of my world with such imaginative depth.

I walked up to Wile and gave him a hug. With him was his wife and one of his medical cronies. "Dr. Wile," I said, "do you remember that day?" He smiled and said he did. And his old friend eyed us with a twinkle of perversity at the mention of *that day*, as if the only thing a young girl and an old man have in common is foreboding. "You talked about love," I said. "And you know what?" he answered, "As I recall, you handled the transitions beautifully." "I did?" I gasped, astonished, and wondering at the same time if the skewed feelings of the past would magically come together if I just believed him now. "Yes, you did," he said. And at that moment I felt that things did come together somehow. That I had gotten what I wanted from him that day; Dr. Wile had given me a ticket for a journey that he knew I wasn't ready to make–but one he realized I had to–perhaps even knowing that one day we would meet again and I could look him in the eye and say, "Made it, Doc."

–Laurie Marks

When a woman speaks her truth, fires up her intention and feeling, stays tight with the instinctive nature, she is singing, she is living in the wild breath-stream of the soul.

–Clarissa Pinkola Estes, PhD,
Women Who Run With the Wolves:
Myths and Stories of the Wild Woman Archetype
(Ballantine Books, New York, 1992, pg. 291).

Chapter Twelve

Spiritual Moments in a Woman's Life

Recently, I had a conversation with a woman who is very close to me. We were discussing what spirituality meant to each of us. She recoiled at my use of the word, "spirituality," and adamantly denied that she even had a spiritual life. I thought her response was particularly odd since I see her spiritual side in her paintings and her sketches.

I can understand why she felt so alienated, yet I think the problem for her was that she was equating spirituality with religion. She didn't realize that spirituality does not have to be a part of organized religion unless you choose it to be so. Most organized religions do not make room for women, and they deny women their power and their abilities to weave magic. It is no wonder that so many women have turned their backs on religion. We must retrieve our lost spirits whether we enlist the aid of religion or not. We must create a woman's way.

The return of the Goddess into the world's consciousness is something to behold. Her return has created the beginnings of a radical shift in perspectives. Women everywhere are learning how to reclaim the Goddess, or the true feminine nature in their own lives. I think this is so important, particularly because I have felt that I, too, am on my own voyage to spiritual awareness, and I haven't known where to turn. I couldn't find the right role models, the right recipes, the right road. I know now that I have to create my own way.

When I think about my own spirituality, I am immediately struck by the feelings it brings to me. I feel spirited, full of my own spirit and intention, connected, fluid, alive, and authentic. This feeling needn't take place on a mountaintop, or walking the beach. True spiritual feelings often occur during times when I am most in tune with myself, when the authentic cord of my life fills me up, when I am at peace with myself. This is my definition, and every woman has her own.

What may move me may not work for you and vice-versa. One of the prevalent myths that is written about in many self-help books is that by following a prescribed spirituality formula, you will automatically experience a spiritual awakening. You are the only one who can know what moves you. You know what experiences you have that make you feel alive, connected, and in touch with your spirit. You are own spiritual guide and don't let anyone tell you differently.

DIRECTIONS

Take out a sheet of paper and on it, I would like you to write down the activities that you engage in which make you feel whole, which make you feel in sync with yourself . . . spiritual. Do not make the mistake of thinking that the only way you can experience these moments is by engaging in formal religious rituals, for although this may be the case for you, it doesn't have to be. Write down what is true for you.

When you are finished, I want you to look at your list, and on the margin, write down the year that the experience occurred. Choose one event and write for twenty minutes or longer about a spiritual experience in your life. Some women find it helpful to write about their first awareness of something larger than themselves. Choose whatever you deem appropriate. If you are working with other women, share your work when you have finished. It is important to share your spiritual journeys, to guide each other into the path of the feminine and to support each other along the way.

A woman can lose her spirit, and frequently does, yet she will find it again. Sometimes, her descent into darkness is accompanied by abuse of alcohol, drugs, or food. However, in this descent, there is always something else–a presence if you wish, a companion, if we allow it to be with us. To lose one's spirit is a frightening experience. I know, for I have lived it. This loss of spirit has paradoxically fueled and blocked my creativity.

For some unknown reason, no matter what happens in my life, I am always able to write. Perhaps, because I've always realized that reclaiming my spirituality to rejoin my own feminine source meant that I had to take out my pen and write; not necessarily profound prose, but prose; my prose. I have to remind myself to trust that my pen can help me reclaim my misplaced spirit which has only been set aside, ignored, but never forgotten. I take many long, hot baths, speak with few people, light candles, and pray my way back. This is my spiritual recipe. You have one too.

Experiment, and add what is needed to your essential ingredients; but, after you find out what works for you, share your recipe. Tell other women, tell the women close to you, tell them to tell their women friends. Let us learn to heal ourselves, and in doing so we can heal our daughters and their daughters and their daughters thereafter. "You are part of the women who have lived and loved before you." I hope that you find your way with love and joy.

WOMEN'S VOICES

When enough russet oak leaves spattered the front lawn, I'd drag the big bamboo rake from the garage. It fanned out like a huge paw with outstretched claws and bumped and jarred along the ground, getting stuck on every root and rock. After a couple of good tugs, I'd get it loose and continue dragging until I reached mid-lawn. In transit, a good ridge of leaves would get stuck and speared, enough to get me started.

Raking and gathering until my arms burned from effort, the pile would grow and grow. The sweeps getting bigger and denser until the musty oak leaves were heaped upon heap.

A running jump from the front porch step, a feet-first dive into the crackling pile. Slide and skid dead, lay still, for a moment soaking up the spicy smell. Be gone tired arms and cramped hands, claws from gripping the big bamboo rake. Just me, my crunchy nest, blue Fall sky and tall oak encased in a moment.

–Nancy Wilson

* * *

There have been many dreams of horses throughout my life, and the symbol of Pegasus, the winged white horse, is a powerful image for me. I still don't fully understand why. All I can think of is this: freedom, air power, animal instinct, inner guidance, which I also guide; there's a partnership between inner and outer self. As I ride this winged creature, he cooperates with me when my intention is good. There's a creative energy within. He's my aide, my helper, and he carries me higher. But, we also land on the ground, almost weightlessly. His wings fold elegantly beneath my legs and I straddle his back. In magical realms, we save or liberate somebody. Somehow, he has something to do with spiritual expression, creative practice and unity in *this* realm, the realm of the body, material reality. With him, I feel a sense of unity with my Higher Self, nurturance in a mental sense, expression of the soul in this realm.

–Paula Denman

* * *

I was *so* religious through my childhood and through high school and even through college. And after that, nothing. Oh, I did enjoy going to *Mass* in France and Italy after I left college. I loved the cathedrals, all shapes, all types, all eras. Even the ones that weren't Catholic were staggering in their size and complexity. In Venice, I attended High Mass at St. Mark's for All Soul's Day. I went to the highest of all high masses, saw more Bishops, Archbishops, Priests, and altar boys then I've ever seen in my entire life. Ritual? This was the Las Vegas of Ritual. Incense? This would set off a smoke detector in today's environment. Bells? This was like an entire handbell orchestra. Organ music? This was enough to wake the dead–which seems fitting since it was All Soul's Day. And the Mass was still in Latin so I still knew all the priests' statements and all the responses. Of course, I couldn't understand the readings from the Epistle or the Gospel, let alone the sermon, but that just gave me free time to look around and try to drink it all in. The richness of the brocades in the vestments, the gold on the altar in the candelabra and the communion cup and the sacristy where the holy wafers were stored. The stained glass windows and the statuary and the wood carving. The memorials to the wealthy of the period, long since gone to their eternal sleep.

But holy? Well, I can't say I feel that way–I'm trying to remember how it felt then. I know I was awestruck but I'm not sure I felt holy.

Holy for me is maybe a little more low key–something with a greater aura of serenity. I've always liked the cloister gardens, something about them seems remote, protected from the outside world of trouble and stress. A beautiful green sanctuary where one could commune and meditate and feel at peace.

–Jeanne Dorward

*   *   *

I met God at the Beach one Sunday afternoon while, walking in the sand, sinking, cold and firm under my shoes, scanning miles of imprints, all shapes, textures and sizes, forming a chaotic pattern of feet running in all directions. The conversation went something like this:

"I wonder who belongs to each footprint; I share the same space and experience with thousands before me, enacting the same rhythmic ritual, breathing, pondering, deciding with gentle introspection."

Stepping with deliberation, head down, eyes darting, the questions came, as each imprint caught my eye.

"Where do they live? What do they look like? What are their burdens, their joys? Who is their mate? Do they have children? What is their age? What are their special gifts and talents? Do they even know? Are they lonely? What do they do for a living? Do they have a family? Are they scared of anything? What are their insecurities, their accomplishments? What pain do they carry? What kind of voice do they have? Do they like to sing? Do they believe in God? What brought them to this stretch of land? Where are they now? Are they happy?"

Touched by the clarity of the moment and my bond to other soulmates, overwhelmed by their presence in this sacred moment, and the thing (or things) we have in common, I concluded with a peaceful sigh and one final question. . . .

"Isn't life wonderful?" The answer finally came.

–Mary Ellen Rescigno

*   *   *

I have crossed quite a few realms of spirituality. From churches to sweat lodges to yoga retreats and finally, zen centers. It has been very rare for me to find any real sense of holiness in these places, peacefulness perhaps.

The time in my life in which I connected to this place seems to have sprung forth from myself. But, it has come to me in a single moment where perhaps I am sitting beside a stream surrounded by the richness of trees standing there as if they knew the answer to what I am not sure. And as the stream moves past, full of life, it offers some reassurance of direction, as if it knows where it is supposed to go. If one could learn to swim with the tide, the flow, instead of against it.

I breathe deeply and when I am in a place where the air is clean, I feel my body being invigorated. My breath brings me back to life and I enjoy it again which I seem to have forgotten to do. My buttocks are cold on the hard ground that holds me. But, it is firm and strong and when I can, I implant myself into the place as if I am part of it. There is no separation that whether I were alive or dead, my spirit would be right there on the earth. That to me is a special place, a place of healing. When I have reached that place in myself, I have touched a spiritual world.

–Julie Butler

*   *   *

Dusk. I walk away from the house, past the mailbox, across the dirt road. My arms are now around the posts of the fence and the wooden gate. I squeeze just enough and I can lift the wire loop from the top and ease through the opening.

Sounds. Horses snorting at the far end of the pasture; the meadowlark's call; water rushing down the hill through the wooden irrigation trough. I walk on up the hill until I can look back and down at the lights in the house. I sit here and watch for the first star and sing-song the nursery rhyme under my breath–"Star light, star bright, I wish I may. . . " and become again still, lying back against the prickly warm earth, smelling the musty richness of dry cow dung. I listen to my breath and am drawn higher and deeper into the sparkled black night. I feel the largeness of my world, feel myself dissolving into the vastness, being one with the stars, knowing the world beyond this self. Knowing that I am safe here, beyond the barriers of fear and loneliness.

–Jyoti Haney

*   *   *

What stood out the most that day was the rain. Of course it always rained in Florida. But this was one of those weird rains, where it was raining in the backyard, but not in the front.

We'd been on a family outing, and as we slowly pulled into the driveway, the sun was shining again. We stepped out of the car into the hot, humid day. In the cool of the kitchen, my sister ran to peer out the window.

"Look, Look," she cried, "It's raining! It's raining in the back-yard!"

My father, stood behind her, his hands on her small, curly head, smiling in that mischievous way he had, like maybe he was up to something.

The rest of us stood behind him, loyal and patient, waiting, and not even daring to breathe. After a time, he moved away from the window. He looked at us, and started to speak, but instead waved his hand, motioning for us to follow. One by one, we traipsed after him, my mother, my sisters, my brother, and me.

He led us onto the back porch, and there we watched the rain and waited.

"Let's shower," he finally said, "Let's shower in the rain."

We all stood still a minute, dumblike, as though maybe we hadn't heard him correctly.

"Look," he said, frowning, turning grim and annoyed, "No one can see. No one can see through the fence."

With that he turned and went inside. When he came back, he was stark naked and carrying soap. He walked out into the center of the yard, letting the rain wet him, slowly soaping himself, oblivious to the rest of us.

My mother went next, taking off her clothes and going to the center of the yard to join my father.

"You're missing out," he called, frowning at us in our haven on the porch. "Well, do what you want," he said, continuing his bath.

Then my sister broke free, running out into the yard, stripping off her clothes, spinning 'round and 'round, and 'round, laughing and sticking out her tongue to taste the rain.

My younger sister and brother went next, going slow and hesitant, like they weren't really sure. I was the last to go. I felt so self-conscious. I didn't want them to see my body, so I waited until everyone went inside, and when the others were dressed and dry, I walked across the wet, green grass, into the center of the yard, to shower in the rain.

–Rebecca Geiger

*   *   *

When I was fourteen, I thought I heard a call from God to become a nun. I was taught by nuns in black habits with crucifixes dangling at their sides. Their faces, framed in white starched cotton, glowed as they taught geography, history, and religion classes. They knew everything about the whole world as well as about God. I truly thought they shared a secret that made them different and very special. I wanted to be like them. I studied hard, received good grades, and stayed after school to help them. Suddenly, one day, I thought I heard God calling me. I prayed a lot, confessed my sins weekly, and got myself a spiritual advisor.

Father Michael was thirty years old and had the bluest eyes I had ever seen. He wore a cassock and black cowboy boots that always needed a shine. He played volleyball with girls and football with boys. When he said Mass, the tips of his boots stuck out from under his church vestments. His thick black hair was a little longer than the other priests'. Looking at Father Michael's wind-burned face as he said Mass, I thought that Jesus must look like this.

Because he was my spiritual advisor, I was asked to help Father Michael with a number of things before and after school. I sorted church mail, stuffed envelopes, and mended torn pamphlets and catechisms. Each morning, I went to the office in the back of the church and began my tasks. I never saw Father Michael until just before I was finished. Then, he quietly appeared in the doorway. Sometimes I never knew he was in the room before I saw him. But I never said anything until he asked me a question. We talked a lot about my vocation. He thought I was too young (to be a nun). I told him that I did not think he was a good priest because he did not encourage me. We had many arguments. I cried. He moved closer to me. I could smell soap and Aqua Velva after-shave lotion. His cassock tickled the backs of my legs. I remembered the bottle of Aqua Velva I had seen at the store. It was the color of Father Michael's eyes.

When I stayed after school to help him, Father Michael took me home in his red Mustang. We talked about a lot of things–my parents, President Kennedy, my younger brothers. Sometimes we didn't say anything to each other. Instead, he would sing a hymn in Latin. He would begin softly, then slowly sing louder and louder until his rich beautiful voice filled the car, spilling out the windows and sank gently down into my shoes. My little girl heart loved Father Michael and Jesus very much that year.

–Joyce Roschinger

* * *

Lost
In the tangled skein
Of my self,
You are the poem
Awakening my soul.
Holding you,
The stars come down
Out of the heavens
To bloom
In my being,
And the ephemeral
Now has been
Found.

–Zoe Smith

* * *

I am a woman who has lived in blankness, hungry for images, both within myself and without. I have spent much of my life in a vacuum, driving myself to keep up appearances, to achieve, to produce, not because these activities were fulfilling, but because I was desperately empty. Even now, relatively secure in the knowledge that I am in the midst of a spiritual awakening, I wrestle with bouts of such acute fear and shame that I lose heart. I have come to know that my struggle is not unique; it is simply a woman's territory in our culture. Years of isolation and disconnection from other women have formed the backdrop of my existence. A compulsive need for secrecy has accompanied my internalized shame, thus I carried immense fear of being found out, of having my worthlessness made known, particularly in the presence of women who appeared to be liberated, who seemed to have it "all together." Profound relief has companioned me in my gradual discovery of deep connections with other women; to validate our experiences together provides a starting point for my spiritual quest in search of the Feminine Divine. . . . To be a woman, I must confront my own namelessness; and, if I stop outside of the parameters of my culturally assigned roles, then who am I? Carol Christ has provided a name for my interior blankness: nothingness, but it is a pregnant state of depth and transformation in which I am invited to be the Queen of my own underworld.

There were patches of light though amidst the bleakness, and like a plant stretching plaintively to catch the sun's life-giving rays, so was I. May was the Blessed Mother's month and I set up a card table in the corner of my bedroom: my altars became such a source of delight. Adding new flowers and rearranging the pieces were such comforting, life-giving tasks. How precious was the space devoted to that special someone of my own kind, a respite from my exile as a girl child. Mary presented one facet of the Goddess of Many Names and, with her gentle womanly presence, my estrangement from myself was lifted, if only for lovely stretches of time. I am filled with gratitude to have her.

–Suzanne Chaumont

* * *

Once again I was looking out the window–always looking. Splashes and smudges of green swooshed by my face. If I refocused my gaze, adjusting it slightly to the next layer of foliage, I could see the details of the forest. The sturdy, gray-green trunks, smooth and slender and young looking; the larger, older trees behind those. They called to me. The forest called my name. "Come be with us . . . ," they beckoned and seduced me, their long arms and hands waving to me, drawing me in, gesturing to me to come closer. They whispered to me. "Come, be one with us . . . . " They rustled and flicked their leaves and made them sparkle in the patchwork of sunlight. I blinked to rest my eyes, and the voices stopped. The blur of the trees moving by resumed. I looked deeper into the forest, but they were still. They didn't call, but waited silently for me to realize that I belonged there with them. "Come be with us. . . , " I heard a voice inside me chant. "Come, be one with us." I kept looking out the window for the remainder of the drive. I remembered how this had brought me comfort as a little girl. I would disappear into the woods and not be affected by anything around me. I would sit by the window at home, and stare out at the green, and meditate silently with the trees as my guide. This is where my soul lives. This is my sanctuary; it always has been. But I'd forgotten to look out the window, and I'd lost myself. Maybe I lost myself the day they cut down my favorite twin oak in the front yard. . . the one outside the picture window.

—Mary Ellen Rescigno

* * *

After the rector had blessed the silver boat and its contents, and all of us standing around the thurible in the dimly lit, cramped vestry with the candlelight flickering across our faces or across the soft pleats of the white robes hanging on pegs in the open-doored armoir, then, after Father Jersey or Father Linz lifted his arm, regal in his robes, to rest his hand on our shoulder, he would usher us out into the hall to the heavy carved oak doors that led into the church from the sacristy, to pause for a few moments before the doors swing wide and the organist began the first trumpeting notes of the hymn.

There were times when my father, my own father, my mother's husband, was in the vestry with us, wearing the Rector's regal apparel, his robe brushing the tops of his shoes. He seemed solid and boxy, but graceful, too. Perhaps because he was encased in so many thickly embroidered layers, it made it rather difficult to move swiftly. My brother or my sister in their dark robes were there sometimes too, clutching their candles, their breath bending and snapping the flame that was wavering just below their chins. This day, my family sat together in the congregation and I wished that one of them had been there to ease some of the inevitable stage-fright anxieties, and so I could ask once again, "After the Eucharist, do I genuflect on my right knee or my left knee, and then do I go into the sacristy or do I go straight up to the altar?" It was always this way, even though I knew perfectly well that no matter what happened, there were people near me at all times that would direct me. My feet also knew the routine and my ears knew the song-pitch cues of the minister's voice and the organ's notes. As Father Jersey and Father Linz and the others were being vested, I could hear the ministers and assistants through the open door of the vestry, as they joked and talked in low, hushed tones so their voices wouldn't travel down the hall, or echo between the oak doors and the jam, or float through the Baptistery and play off the huge vaulted ceilings of the church. I was reassured though, because there was humor and tenderness in this ritual, and not the rigidity that I was expecting.

I found my mother among the congregation and tried not to smile. Father Jersey's twisted cincture had set the tone for the service. It was two weeks until Easter and amity was in the air, along with the first damp, woody scents of a new and early spring. Like an ether, the prospect of spring made people giddy after a brutal New England winter, and the congregation was not immune to it. Or maybe it was the incense, the way it filled our nostrils and our lungs, too.

It, like spring, was often musky but it had a bitter sting. As a child, I liked the smell of the more acerbic incense the way I liked the smell of spilled gasoline at a gas station, or the momentary bite of cigarette smoke on the train.

The Lady Chapel was ablaze with flowers "given to the glory of God and in the loving memory of . . . . " Out of the corner of my eye I saw the organist lift his arms in mock exaggeration as he attempted to attract the attention of the choir, and then place his hands deliberately on the organ keys. I told my father when I was much younger that I wanted to sing in the church choir. When I sang loud enough for him to hear me when he was standing next to me in church, then, "this would be a good time to join the choir . . . , " he advised. Since his hearing rapidly became worse, my strong singing was never acknowledged and became a source of quiet frustration until I reached an age where singing in the church choir was not as pressing as other pursuits. On this particular Sunday, however, I sang along with the choir, alone in my single altar pew. The choir voices served as impetus for me to sing with abandon, and I did. I lost myself to the sound of song echoing off the cavernous vaulted ceiling, and sweeping up into the bell tower, and reverberating off the big, melancholy bells.

–Elizabeth Day

Closing

I hope that *The Way of the Woman Writer* has inspired you to write your truths, and your life stories with ease. The writing exercises are only a beginning and I encourage you to use your writing, your words, and your reflections as a stepping-off point for further work. You may wish to begin a writing group with some friends and conduct the writing exercises with other women of like mind. Perhaps, you have ignited a passion for writing that will lead you to writing articles, or books, or taking classes at local universities.

The writing world is a solitary world—yet it needn't be. I encourage you to write as the spirit moves you and to share your work with supportive family people. Your stories count, your feelings count, and it is my wish that your words will lead you to be the woman that you wish to be.

Let your writing urge you, deepen your feelings, disturb you, and lead you to your inner truths.

Everyone has a story to tell and I hope that the documentation of your story has given you strength, hope, inspiration, and joy.

I honor all of you who have the courage to write your stories.

* * *

I am happy to receive your comments about this book. If you wish to contact me or to write to any of the women who contributed to the writing in this book, please send your note to:

Janet Lynn Roseman
c/o The Haworth Press Book Division
10 Alice Street
Binghamton, NY 13904-1580

The list of resources at the back of the book will provide you with additional sources of information about writing. Although there are many, many good books on writing on the market, I am listing the books that I have read and am familiar with. I encourage you to visit your favorite library, go to used bookstores and build your own writing library.

Additional resources include lists of writing organizations which you may find helpful. Write to the organizations that interest you and then make up your mind which groups you wish to align yourself with. Trust yourself. You will find the way of the woman writer. Your way.

CONTRIBUTORS

Fran (Neenie) Bradford. Gore Vidal notes that "few men have the energy or capacity to successfully conduct more than one career in a lifetime." Writing is my fourth and I wonder why and how this happens to be so.

Julie Butler is 30 years old. She is presently living in Baltimore, Maryland and works for a graphic artist. She is taking creative writing classes and hopes to write a book on "Women in the 90s." Her interests are karate, reading, dancing, friends, and finding work with meaning.

Kathleen Byrne. I have always written—poetry, reports, lists, letters, dreams, cards, journals, and letters. But I have not always been a writer. That distinction came with the recent recognition that my words are important and inevitable, meaningful and mine to share.

Suzanne P. Chaumont holds a Master of Arts degree from the Institute for Culture and Creation Spirituality in Oakland, California. She is an educator, counselor, and facilitator.

Shelly Compton first fell in love with story as a child in Texas and has only recently rediscovered her voice after a long silence, and is now writing with a fury. She has been, over the years, a drifter, a gypsy, a fortune teller, a dreamer, and a teller of tales. Above all, she has been one who listens. Currently, she is a mom and works on a magazine in San Francisco.

Cary Davis makes her living these days as an artist, creating unusual jewelry from objects found on the streets of San Francisco and nearby beaches. At different points in her life, she has taught high school English in Arizona and sold real estate in Georgia. Next on her agenda is earning a master's degree in Rehabilitation Counseling, bringing years of volunteer work to fruition, and hopefully

143

working with women and families of women with osteoporosis. Then, she hopes to settle in the desert with her husband and get back to the serious business of art, and possibly a little writing, a dog, and a garden.

After living in San Francisco for three years and spending seven months traveling in Eastern and Western Europe and Africa, *Elizabeth Day* returned to Boston where she was born in 1967. In 1989, she graduated from the University of Pennsylvania with a major in history in the hopes of one day integrating history and fiction. She is now busy writing about the challenging and illuminating experiences she had on the road.

Paula Denman is a writer, artist, and emerging multi-media producer living and working in San Francisco. She has worked professionally as a fine and commercial artist, writer, photographer, movie-maker, and teacher. She is the owner and founder of Innerface Creative Services, a scriptwriting and storyboard illustration service.

After a twenty-year hiatus, *Jeanne Dorward* is exploring her universe through writing. Originally interested in poetry, she has chosen autobiographical and first-person writing as her means for self-expression. Jeanne also draws on her love for travel as a subject for her vignettes. She asks patience and compassion from her readers and tries to grant herself the same.

Rebecca Geiger is a San Francisco writer, currently able to pay the rent by working as a researcher at *Parenting Magazine.* In her free time, she swims, reads, and takes long walks. She has no cats.

Jyoti Haney descends from pioneers that left the way of wealth in the Old Country to come West and homestead in the rugged mountains of Montana. She, in turn, left the material wealth of a career in Southern California to journey solo to Japan, Nepal, and India on a quest for a different way of being in the world. Writing to her is a continuing solo journey–a pilgrimage to the sacred sites of the inner landscape; an encounter with the spareness of her own "third world." Her name "Jyoti" was a gift from the Nepalese and Indians who heard her former nickname, "Jodie" as this Sanskrit word for

Light. She is currently living in Berkeley, California, where she has a rewarding practice in bioenergy balancing.

Ruth Hynds is a painter and watercolorist who finds words bubbling up to be recorded and images demanding to be painted when she writes.

A native New Yorker, *Susan Karp* has been writing since the age of eight, when she discovered the rhyming properties of "house" and "mouse." Countless words later, she now works as a copywriter and lives in San Francisco.

Rhoda London has a M.F.A. with distinction from the California College of Arts and Crafts. She has exhibited in galleries and museums in California and abroad. She is an integral force in the Institute for Living Arts in San Francisco and the local chapter of the Women's Caucus for Art. An experienced curator, she was responsible for the provocative exhibition "Telling Stories: Artists' Books and Journals," which gave countless women the opportunity to share their stories.

Laurie Marks lives in Oakland, California with three furry cats, one husband, and about a trillion story ideas. She currently works as a sales rep for a large New York publishing company.

"Dear Brian Hopkins, I Love You. Love, *Mary Ellen Rescigno*." This was the beginning of my life as a writer in the second grade, on a tiny square of white school paper. Diaries, journals, detailing my every thought and emotion, poems, stories, inspired verse, prayers, more journals, recording my view of the world, a children's book, songs, more journals, and an autobiography-in-progress. At age 36, I call myself a writer. Oh, by the way, I began writing in Thornwood, New York. (You've never heard of it . . . I know.) I currently write in Alameda, California.

Jovita Angulo AKA: *Joyce Roschinger* has a degree from San Francisco State University in Creative Writing. She has been in hospital management for 12 years. She is currently at work on a book of letters from her father. She lives with her husband in San Francisco.

Zoe Chew Smith. The greatest gifts I have received in my lifetime are those of birth, death, and relationship. Writing connects and transforms these experiences into soul-felt expression. I live in a tiny, remote, northern California town and am nurtured by the hills, sea, solitude, walking, birding, quilting, and life with my husband, daughter, and familiars.

Sandra Stevens attended the Atlanta College of Art before moving to San Francisco to pursue photography and writing. She is currently writing a book about prostitution in the Bay Area.

Nancy Wilson. I come from a long line of curmudgeons, crackpots, and Connecticut Yankees. Writing is still my means of escape.

READING LIST

Anderson, Sherry Ruth and Hopkins, Patricia (1991) *The Feminine Face of God: The Unfolding of the Sacred in Women*, New York, Bantam Books.

Bateson, Mary Catherine (1990) *Composing a Life*, New York, A Plume Book.

Baldwin, Christina (1991) *Life's Companion: Journal Writing as a Spiritual Quest*, New York, Bantam Books.

Brande, Dorothea (1934) *Becoming a Writer*, Los Angeles, J.P. Tarcher.

Carlson, Kathie (1990) *In Her Image: The Unhealed Daughter's Search for Her Mother*, Boston, Shambhala.

Chamberlain, Mary (1988) *Writing Lives: Conversations Between Women Writers*, London, Virago Press.

Dillard, Annie (1989) *The Writing Life*, New York, Harper and Row.

Duerk, Judith (1989) *Circle of Stones: Woman's Journey to Herself*, San Diego, Luramedia.

Estes, Clarissa Pinkola, PhD (1992) *Women Who Run with the Wolves: Myths and Stories of the Wild Woman Archetype*, New York, Ballantine Books.

Goldberg, N. (1986) *Writing Down the Bones: Freeing the Writer Within*, Boston, Shambhala.

Harris, Maria (1989) *Dance of the Spirit: The Seven Stages of Women's Spirituality*, New York, Bantam Books.

Heilbrun, E.G. (1988) *Writing a Woman's Life*, New York, W.W. Norton.

Henri, Robert (1923) *The Art Spirit*, New York, Harper and Row.

Metzger, Deena (1992) *Writing for Your Life: A Guide and Companion to the Inner Worlds*, San Francisco, Harper.

Murdock, Maureen (1990) *The Heroine's Journey*, Boston, Shambhala.

Noble, Vicki (1991) *Shakti Woman: Feeling Our Fire, Healing Our World, The New Female Shamanism*, San Francisco, Harper.

Noble, Vicki (1993) *Uncoiling the Snake: Ancient Patterns in Contemporary Women's Lives*, San Francisco, Harper.

Rosenwasser, Penny (1992) *Visionary Voices: Women on Power*, San Francisco, Aunt Lute Books.

Saunders, Lesley (1987) *Glancing Fires: An Investigation into Women's Creativity*, London, The Women's Press.

Stark, Freya (1936) *The Journey's Echo*, New York, The Ecco Press.

Sternburg, J. (1980) *The Writer on Her Work, Volume I and II*, New York, W.W. Norton and Co.

Ueland, Brenda (1938) *If You Want to Write: A Book About Art, Independence, and Spirit*, St. Paul, Graywolf Press.

Wakefield, Dan (1990) *The Story of Your Life: Writing a Spiritual Autobiography*, Boston, Beacon Press.

Woolf, Virginia (1929) *A Room of One's Own*, New York, Harcourt, Brace, Jovanovich.

Woodman, Marion, (1985) *The Pregnant Virgin: A Process of Psychological Transformation*, Toronto, Canada, Inner City Books.

Woodman, Marion (1993) *Leaving My Father's House: A Journey to Conscious Femininity*, Boston, Shambhala.

Woodman, Marion (1993) *Conscious Femininity: Interviews with Marion Woodman*, Toronto, Canada, Inner City Books.

WRITING ORGANIZATIONS

American Society of Journalists and Authors
Suite 302
1501 Broadway
New York, New York 10036

Associated Writing Programs
Old Dominion University
Norfolk, Virginia 23529

The Author's Guild
330 W. 42nd Street
New York, New York 10036

The Dramatists' Guild
234 W. 44th Street
New York, New York 10036

International Women's Writing Guild
P.O. Box 810
Gracie Station
New York, New York 10028

National Writers Union
13 Astor Place
New York, New York 10003

PEN American Center
568 Broadway
New York, New York 10012

Poets and Writers
72 Spring Street
New York, New York 10012

Index